THE BOWDEN WAY

50 YEARS OF LEADERSHIP WISDOM

BOBBY BOWDEN

WITH STEVE BOWDEN

LONGSTREET PRESS

Atlanta

Published by
LONGSTREET PRESS, INC.
2974 Hardman Court
Atlanta, Georgia 30305

Printed in the United States of America

1st printing, paperback, 2002

Library of Congress Catalog Card Number: 2001091247

ISBN: 1-56352-703-0

Jacket and book design by Burtch Hunter Design LLC

CONTENTS

FOREWORD
FOR THE PAPERBACK EDITION

You CAN'T TEACH EXPERIENCE.

That's the one great lesson illustrated in our 8-4 season of 2001.

The 2001 season ended a lot of streaks for us. Most consecutive final rankings in the Top 5—gone. Most consecutive ten-win seasons—gone. Longest home game undefeated streak—gone. League championships every year since entering the ACC – gone. Fifteen straight New Year's Day games—gone.

Fortunately, we coaches saw it coming. Not that we planned on losing four games. Our goal was to win all twelve. But tragedy and hardship hit our team hard before the season ever began.

The tragedy was the death of Devaughn Darling, a linebacker who died of heart complications during winter conditioning drills in February, 2001. Coaches, players and I were all devastated. Heartache and a sense of uncertainty burdened us throughout the season.

Next, when we reported in August for our season preparations, four starters were lost to season-ending injuries. The losses were huge. We graduated 14 starters from our 2000 team. Those guys took us to the National Championship Game for three straight years, winning it wire-to-wire in 2000! That left only eight returning starters, which is always scary. August injuries cut those numbers down to four. And the consequence was that we had to rely on a large number of inexperienced freshmen and red-shirt freshmen to help lead our team. Of paramount concern to me was that our starting quarterback, a redshirt freshman, had never played a down of college football.

Lack of experience affects the way coaches coach and players play. We coaches were forced to limit the number of formations and plays we could use on offense and defense. The defensive coordinator, for example, couldn't blitz as much as he would've preferred. Why? Because our young, inexperienced cornerbacks couldn't provide consistent man-to-man coverage on the outside. The defense played a lot of predictable zone coverages, which our stronger opponents exploited. Our offensive coordinator, to cite another example, had to limit our quarterback's freedom to audible at the line of scrimmage, owing to the freshman's inexperience in reading opposing defenses or recognizing a disguised blitz. As a result, we often stayed with a running play even when opposing defenses suddenly put nine men up front to stop it. When we did gamble with blitzes and audibles, we usually got burned. It was a real catch-22 dilemma for coaches and players alike.

What we lacked during the 2001 season was the one thing a coach cannot teach—*EXPERIENCE!*

Experience comes only with time. It's that simple.

In any business or organizational endeavor, when adversity strikes – particularly when the organization loses senior leadership and is left with a high percentage of inexperienced employees or colleagues to run the show – one must circle the wagons, reduce the size of the playbook, and focus on the few things your organization can do well. As experience increases, so can the playbook.

Does such a simple stop-gap strategy guarantee success?

Nope, but it can protect against failure.

Does it mean you can conceal your weaknesses?

Not necessarily, and not against a seasoned adversary.

But if your plan is adapted to your circumstances, and if you are surrounded by good people, you can weather the storm sufficiently until experience is gained.

That's why I'm so excited about this 2002 season. Our team is still young. But the guys have a year of experience under their belts. And our four injured players are back on the field.

I'll leave you with one final thought.

A skilled dog trainer once remarked: *If you can't teach a dog to do what you want him to do, then teach him to do what he can do.*

That's good advice for any leader . . . especially for one who must preside over an inexperienced team.

BOBBY BOWDEN
AUGUST 2002

FOREWORD

Asking Bobby Bowden to offer pointers on leadership has a certain ironic quality. After all, a great leader is a lot like a great football player. Once you get him pointed in the right direction, you sit back to see what happens next. The flow of events can be very creative. And the results are usually the stuff of highlight reels.

Coach Bowden has thrived in one of the most demanding professions of our era. And he has built successful football programs for over 50 years. Many of his accomplishments are unparalleled and have been achieved under remarkable circumstances. Yet he's praised as much for his moral convictions as for his professional achievements.

I prevailed upon Coach Bowden to write this book because he is a leader in every important sense of the term. He is also flawed and imperfect. Bobby Bowden will readily confess his fallibility, and he prefers the word *lucky* in place of *successful*. He and I must be content to disagree on the impact of Lady Luck. He demurs unnecessarily. I have the facts on my side!

Coach Bowden has been a winner wherever he has coached.

In the decade of the 1990s, his teams won more football games than any other Division I school, posting a cumulative record of 110-13-1. Florida State won undisputed national championships in 1993 and 1999. In 2000, the NCAA officially declared his program a "dynasty." Currently second only to Joe Paterno of Penn State for most wins by an active coach, he is on track to surpass the legendary Paul "Bear" Bryant as the winningest coach in the history of Division I football.

Coach Bowden's success in building winning programs did not begin at Florida State. Wherever he's been in charge, he has been successful. Consider his record at each school where he has served as head coach:

YEARS	SCHOOL	RECORD
1955-59	South Georgia Junior College	22-11
1959-63	Samford University	31-6
1970-75	West Virginia University	42-26
1976-2000	Florida State University	243-55-4

Ask yourself how many start-up businesses are successful year in and year out, without any major setbacks, and you begin to put these numbers in perspective. Ask how many publicly traded companies post positive earnings year after year, even in a bear market, and you get even more perspective. Coach Bowden's ability to build winning programs is unsurpassed.

Consider, also, that in bowl games, where great teams consistently duel with other great teams, Bobby Bowden has the highest winning percentage in the history of college football.

Leadership is the key ingredient Coach Bowden brings to coaching. His career began at a small junior college in south Georgia. There he won games and built a successful program. The trend continued at Howard College (now Samford University), where he held the record for most wins until son Terry broke his record in 1992. His first Division I assignment was at West Virginia University. Despite scant resources and an imposing schedule of competition, he consistently won again. And now at FSU, where he's been steering the same ship for 26 years, his program is annually one of the best in college football.

Whatever leadership style he has developed, it works.

And the dynamics of leadership don't change all that much when we shift from the football field to the corporate board room or the sales manager's office. One must work with others – and thereby lead others – to conceive, implement and maintain a successful plan.

Like so many others who find themselves in positions of responsibility, Coach Bowden did not appear on the scene as a ready-made leader. No one trained him for the task. He had the examples of those who went before him. He had the benefit of his upbringing. He had a devout religious faith and a passion for football. But the remainder of his reputation – indeed the lion's share – was forged in the refining fire of life's daily experiences.

In addition to drawing on his own experiences, Coach Bowden has long been a student of military history. He pores over the biographies of well-known generals of the modern era – all great leaders who accomplished great things on the battlefield – including Bonaparte, Grant, Lee, Jackson, Patton, Rommel, Eisenhower, and MacArthur. He studies their lives to learn how they accomplished things . . . how they got things done . . . and what strategies they employed in particular circumstances. For instance, when Patton faced Rommel in the African desert, he had to deploy his reserve troops in such a way as to defend against a breakthrough by Rommel's tanks. A breakthrough could happen anywhere along his front line, and maybe in more than one place. The use of reserves would be a key to Rommel's defeat. So what went into Patton's thinking? What did he know about Rommel that allowed him to hope for victory against a superior foe? And what did he do with those reserves?

Coach Bowden likes to get inside the minds of these great generals and think their thoughts. The lessons he's learned have long been part of his leadership strategy – including the way he prepares his reserve players on offense and defense!

This book turns the tables on Coach Bowden by allowing the reader to get inside *his* head. How does Coach Bowden solve problems? What are his strategies for the particular circumstances he faces? And what has he learned after 50 years in coaching?

The following chapters are his answers to these questions.

By the way, I'm Coach Bowden's son.

It's a plus, because he can't blow any smoke around me. And, no, he doesn't make me call him "Coach Bowden." At least not all the time!

R. Stephen Bowden

INTRODUCTION

I've already made the journey. I know what's ahead of you.

I'm old-fashioned.

I intend to stay that way.

But let me tell you what I mean by *old-fashioned.*

Some truths persist through time. Some ways of doing things continue to work decade after decade, and century after century. Minor adjustments might be required along the way, but the basic recipe is still good.

My recipe for leadership existed long before I came on the scene. I just borrowed and adapted it for coaching. In every job I've held as a head coach, I have used this recipe to help build my program. I believe in it. It hasn't failed me yet. And if I was starting my career anew in the 21st century, I'd use it all over again.

That's what I mean by old-fashioned.

Of course, I've tinkered with the recipe during the past 50 years. That's unavoidable. Times change, and so must we. Old truths must be applied to new situations. But with each successful application, the old truths are reaffirmed.

The world has changed a lot since I was a child. My parents were born in the horse-and-buggy days, and they died in the space age. I was a young teenager during WWII. I've lived to witness atomic fission, men on the moon, the dissolution of the Soviet Union, the rise of genetic engineering, and the advent of a new technological millennium. I doubt human history has ever witnessed more change than what has happened during my lifetime.

Yet the basics of good leadership don't seem to have changed at all.

Like lemonade, chocolate pie, and home-cooked meals, the really good stuff endures.

1
HAVING A GAME PLAN

←——————————————————→

I've never had a 10-year plan or a five-year plan.
I have a one-year plan, and the plan hasn't
varied much over the years.

A seasoned coach knows better than to plan too far ahead. Coaches are evaluated at the end of each season. It's a one-year window to improve or diminish your job security. So you sink roots in the community like you'll be there forever. Then you coach each year like it's your last.

I need a good one-year plan for my coaching career. College administrators can worry about the long-range stuff. If I lose too many ballgames this year, the term *long-range* won't mean much to me. I'll be relegated to "Lone Ranger" status.

Building a successful program boils down to four objectives:

    ✗ Devise a good plan
    ✗ Hire good people to implement the plan
    ✗ Motivate players to buy into the plan
    ✗ Execute the plan.

Football programs operate on an annually recurring cycle. We're not like the manufacturing company that produces widgets day in and day out, 365 days a year. We're more like the seasonal business that must constantly gear up for a few months of heavy sales.

Our "peak season" begins with fall practice in August, continues through the regular season of games, and may extend into early January. Coaches may work 14-16 hour days, sometimes seven days a week, during peak season. Recruiting comes next. Coaches spend most of this time on the road visiting high school athletes. Recruiting season culminates on "signing day" in early February. Next come two and one-half weeks of winter conditioning drills. All current players must participate. Then we gear up for spring ball in March/April. The month of May is dedicated to junior recruiting. Our coaches visit high schools and review the academic transcripts of every player we hope to recruit next year. June is our slow month, usually reserved for family vacations and relaxed office hours. For me, it's the time when my sons and I sponsor the Bowden football camp, which I squeeze in between golf charities and banquets, banquets, banquets. By early July we're all back in the office. My coaches sponsor a week-long football camp at FSU for interested teenagers, and we spend the rest of the month gearing up for the start of a new season. The cycle continues year after year.

Of course, I make our work-year sound compartmentalized. It's really not that way. We watch game film year-round whenever we have the opportunity. We film each day of spring practice, and our coaches review the film each evening before the next day's practice. In July, we begin viewing film on our upcoming opponents. Each coach must submit a scouting report to me by July 15. These reports cover every upcoming opponent and include film breakdowns, articles, write-ups, and any other information pertinent to our efforts. We all watch film daily during the regular season.

Recruiting is also a year-round process. We begin in March with a list of over 500 high school juniors around the country that we're interested in. Our coaches visit those students' schools in the month of May. By August, we pare that list down to 100 players, all of whom are now entering their senior year. By December, we get it down to 50 and hit the ground running. We aggressively recruit those 50 players right up until signing day in February. When the smoke clears, we will have signed 20-25 new players to a scholarship. Then the recruiting coordinator goes back to work getting another list of 500 prospects for the upcoming year, while pulling in transcripts, test scores, recommendations on prospects, and all the other details related to application for admission at FSU.

This cycle of activity is typical of any major college football program. The question is, *Can I manage these activities well enough to field a good team and win on Saturdays?*

Here's what it comes down to for me:

DEVISE A GOOD PLAN

I've just given you the basic plan that we follow year after year.

But I'm a stickler for detail. I want to fine-tune that plan each year. My staff and I must all be on the same page regarding our assignments, responsibilities, and expectations. So here's what I do.

I schedule what we call a *hideaway* each year at the end of July. My coaches and I carve out five days, Monday through Friday, to be alone together. We pick a location – such as Destin, Florida – and *hide away* from all the distractions of the office.

Hideaway is for strategic and tactical planning. A copy of my hideaway notes is distributed to each coach. The document is over 100 pages long. I will not divulge any details of this document, except to say it's a comprehensive overview of everything we aim to do in the coming year.

We cover different topics on each day of hideaway. When hideaway ends on Friday, we're all on the same page. Priorities have been established. Responsibilities have been delegated. Calendars are coordinated. And each coach knows what is expected of him. We've got a well-honed plan for the upcoming year.

You'll find numerous references in this book to our annual hideaway meeting. This event is one of my most essential management tools.

HIRE GOOD PEOPLE TO IMPLEMENT THE PLAN

Good plans are only as good as the people who implement them. I firmly believe that my coaching staff is a major reason for our remarkable success at FSU. People may think our success is due to great players, but we won before we had great players. People may think it's because FSU invested millions into our athletic facilities, but we won before we had decent facilities. We won because we had great coaches who worked hard, completed their assignments, and knew how to get the most out of our limited resources.

If a leader does not surround himself with good people, he'll spend most of his time swimming against the current. And somewhere along the way, he'll drown from exhaustion.

MOTIVATE THE PLAYERS TO BUY INTO THE PLAN

If you can be successful without having to motivate the people down in the trenches, more power to you. It doesn't work that way in college football. If my players aren't motivated to work hard, we won't win.

I hear people say, *Oh, Bobby Bowden doesn't need to motivate his players because, top to bottom, he recruits the best players in the country.*

I wish it were that simple.

Let me suggest that you check out the NBA, the NFL, and the PGA on any given Sunday. Every participant you see is a superior athlete. They are the finest in their sport. Yet some of those teams, and some of those players, don't perform well on game day. In fact, some of them lose consistently. Have you ever wondered why?

I cannot succeed in football unless the players believe in our plan. Every one of them, from All-Americans to third-teamers to non-scholarship players, must buy into the system and contribute individually to the success of our program.

Let me illustrate.

For nine days in February each year, our players go through winter conditioning drills at 6 A.M. These drills are grueling. They are like nothing my players have experienced before. Aside from two-a-day practices in the torrid heat of August, no rigor is more physically demanding.

We call them *mat drills.*

I've conducted mat drills for nearly 50 years. All my sons went through them. And these drills have far more value to me than mere physical conditioning. We build our team on those mats. Players push one another not to drag behind. If a drill is not performed properly, the entire group must repeat the drill. Now trust me, these players don't want to repeat a drill. They hate it when one of their buddies doesn't follow directions or puts in a half-hearted effort. So, despite their exhaustion, the players learn to encourage one another and struggle together. Cohesiveness emerges. Pride of accomplishment is born. And during this process, the coaches discover who the natural teams leaders are – which players work the hardest and motivate the others to push on.

Maybe now you see why our players must buy into the plan. If they don't buy into it, they won't try very hard. And if they don't try hard, none of us will learn enough of what we need to know. It's like a math test. If you don't try your best, how can we know how smart you are?

The same holds true for game-day performance. Players play the way they practice. If a guy loafs during practice, he'll loaf during the game. Take my word for it. It's as certain as the sun. To play their best on game day, our players must believe in the value of each day's practice. They must drive themselves to improve their skills on the practice field.

My job is to motivate them toward that end. Otherwise, we will lose on game day.

EXECUTE THE PLAN

When hideaway ends, we coaches are ready for the upcoming year.

Beginning in August and continuing through the following July, we now must execute our various assignments. We must do our jobs day by day, month by month. That's what we're hired for. Execution puts us in a position to win on the field.

Okay, you say, *so how do you go about doing all those things?*

How do you hire good people?

How do you motivate the people in the trenches?

How do you ensure proper execution?

And what do you do when things go wrong?

The remaining chapters are dedicated to answering those questions. I don't claim that my way is the best way. But my way works for me. It has worked for a long time. So let me tell you what I've learned over the past 50 years.

2
TAKING CHARGE

←——————————————————→

Even when you're wrong, you're still the boss.

My motive for taking charge is elegant in its simplicity: *I like my job and don't want to lose it!*

＊

Here's one insight that every leader should accept at a deep emotional level – namely, EVERYTHING THAT OCCURS WITHIN AN ORGANIZATION REFLECTS BACK UPON ITS LEADER.

If something bad happens on your watch, outsiders will wonder why you weren't watching. If an employee performs poorly, they will ask why you hired that person in the first place. If poor decisions are made that damage your organization's reputation, people will cast a wary glance toward the ultimate decision-maker. Whether or not you should be blamed, you will be.

So you'd better take charge, lest the actions of others get you fired.

The leader is ultimately responsible for all that occurs within the organization. This burden comes with the territory.

Back in 1993, several of our players allowed a sports agent's representative to take them shopping at a local Tallahassee sporting goods store. Both the agent and the players knew the act was a violation of NCAA rules. The story made national headlines.

Now NCAA rules are there for good reason, but they aren't always related to what common sense would tell you is inappropriate. For example, if a friend takes you into a store and buys you a new pair of shoes, you can accept the gift with no problems. The money is not stolen or counterfeit. A fair price is paid for the shoes. There's nothing illegal or immoral about it. You will probably be grateful for the nice gift.

But if a person (who also happens to respresent a sports agent) buys shoes for a college athlete, it's a violation of NCAA rules. That's what happened with a few of our players, and for it, they were punished by suspension from ballgames. The rule exists to help deter a much bigger problem of cheating in athletics, so there's no complaint with the NCAA. And we accepted the punishment without complaint. Our players knew about the rule before they went shopping.

Some writers referred to this episode as "The Foot Locker Scandal." I still fail to see how it qualified for status as an outright scandal, though saying this in print will have some calling for my head. And those writers who called it a "buying spree" have never been shopping with my wife! In her calculus, buying a few pairs of tennis shoes is only a warm-up exercise.

Nonetheless, one of the first public accusations was that I knew this was going on but chose to look the other way. The accusation was false, but it was made nonetheless.

Why?

Because I'm the guy in charge.

It's my responsibility as leader to take prescriptive measures to prevent such episodes. No matter that coaches hate having agents around their players. No matter that coaches and the team suffer when players are suspended. My football program had nothing to gain from condoning these actions. Yet we – and I – were held to blame. People naturally ask of a leader, *Why did this happen on your watch?* In fact, when we told the NCAA we didn't know about it at the time, their response was, *Well, why DIDN'T you know about it?*

I mention this case only to illustrate that, as a leader, you can pass the blame all you want. You can blame your junior officers. You can blame bad luck. You can blame society's lax moral standards. And you may be correct on all counts. But other people will blame *you* because *you're* the person in charge. That's just the way it is.

People expect the leader to lead effectively. It's an appropriate expectation. If improprieties such as the Foot Locker episode occurred frequently, FSU would be justified in firing me. After all, no football recruit can play at Florida State without MY prior approval. The recruiting standards we use are MY standards. And notification of players about NCAA rules is MY ultimate responsibility. That's the way people outside my program view the matter. It's the way every leader is viewed, and it won't ever change.

My advice, then, is to accept the fact that you are ultimately responsible for everything that occurs in your organization. That's why you must take charge and lead with authority. Your neck is on the line.

Lead as if you'll be held accountable, because you will be.

Taking charge doesn't mean you must become a harsh taskmaster. It does mean, however, that you take the initiative and invest the energy to stay on top of things within your organization. Taking charge means hands-on management. It means being *pro*active rather than *re*active. Leaders who take charge send out a message to everyone else – namely, *We have a job to do, and we're going to get it done.*

✳

When you first assume your role as leader, you don't need to harp on the fact that you are in charge. Folks already know. They understand your authority to hire and fire, to promote or demote, to raise their pay or change their job assignments.

So take advantage of the moment. Share your vision for the future. Lay the ground rules that all must follow. Enumerate your expectations. And let them see your resolve to move the organization in a positive direction.

Personally, I think a leader's first day on the job – or the first week, as the case may be – is the best time to speak candidly and let everyone know where you stand. This is the time to set forth the marching orders. Just be sure to stick with the tune you've chosen to play.

When I took the job at Florida State in January 1976, one of my first meetings was with the players. These boys had won only four games under two different coaches in the three previous years. I think they saw me as just another guy the administration brought in to lead them through another losing season. I was determined to change that perception.

Here is an excerpt from that initial encounter. Bear in mind that I am addressing 19- and 20-year-old student-athletes, not middle-aged employees, faculty members, or junior executives. My message would change if the audience was different, but my candor would remain:

Gentlemen, let me explain the importance of why we're all here together.

First of all, we've got to have a basic understanding of who's in charge around here. There can never be a question of that. Well, I am the new guy around here. I'm the head coach. In the past three years your Florida State football team has managed to win only four games, and in the meantime, you lost 29. You tried it your way, and where did it get you?

Nowhere.

Now, I think I know how to win. And from now on at Florida State we will do things my way. If you don't like it, then hit the door. Go somewhere else. Because if winning doesn't mean something to you, then we don't need you. From now on it's going to be an honor to wear a garnet jersey and represent Florida State University. We're going to win again at Florida State.

We can turn this program around, but it will take a big effort by everyone. We must push ourselves harder than ever before. We must make sacrifices — give up individual goals in order to reach a much bigger team goal. But we can do it.

I want you to know what it feels like to be a winner, to be able to walk around this campus with the satisfaction of knowing that 'Yes, we can win.' And in order to get that feeling of confidence, and to begin winning football games, then some things around here have got to change.

First of all, we've got to develop a winning attitude, and that means self-discipline because self-discipline wins football games. . . .

Now in order to . . . develop self-discipline, we've got to make some rules. And that means making a commitment to ourselves and to each other that we're going to follow those rules.

I laid out some of the new rules these players would be expected to follow, and then I concluded:

Now, gentlemen, listen up on this final point. We represent a lot of people . . . our families, our friends back home, and, very important-ly, we represent Florida State University. And as a team I want to point this out to you – YOU'RE NOT ORDINARY. YOU'RE NOT AVERAGE. YOU'RE SOMETHING SPECIAL – and I don't want you to ever forget that.

We have a tough road ahead. We've got to be both mentally and phys-ically tough to make it. But if we're prepared in the proper manner, then when the time comes, winning will take care of itself. [i]

I know what some of my players were thinking. They were won-dering, *Who does this guy think he is?* These players had been the butt of jokes all across campus for years. They had conditioned

---

[i]   *Bound for Glory*, by Bobby Bowden, as told to Mike Bynum. The *We Believe Trust Fund*, College Station, TX, 1980.

themselves to accept defeat. And here I was challenging them to believe what their experience told them would not happen. A few kids quit the team. One or two tested us. The rest understood that things were going to be different. The lingering question, however, was how the players would respond to my leadership when the fall season rolled around.

That fall we lost our opening game 21-12 to Memphis State, then got hammered 47-0 by Miami. My players seemed not to have shaken their loser's mentality. The year was shaping up early as a disaster in the making. To make things worse, Oklahoma was next on the schedule, and they were contending for the national championship. As an extra drop in my cup of sorrows, we had to play them on their home field.

Well, I certainly didn't want to be humiliated by the Sooners. But I also didn't want undependable guys out there on the field representing FSU. So I took one of the biggest gambles of my coaching career. When we took the field in Norman, Oklahoma, seven upperclassmen were benched, and seven inexperienced freshmen lined up in their positions. I was determined to put guys on the field who were hungry to win. They'd probably lose the game, I figured, but at least these freshmen would go down fighting.

Well, we led Oklahoma 9-3 in the second quarter before losing 24-9. And a team was born. The next year these same freshmen (now sophomores) went 10-2 with a victory over Texas Tech in the Tangerine Bowl. Two years later, as seniors, they took an undefeated record into the 1979 Orange Bowl against – who else? – Oklahoma. We lost that game to a superior team. And we lost to Oklahoma again the following year in the same bowl. After that, we didn't lose another bowl game until the end of the 1996 season!

Had I not stuck to my guns and followed through on the message I delivered to those players in January 1976, I'm not sure we would've come through that difficult first year. We didn't succeed due to my brilliance as a coach. But I knew only one way to coach – only one way that I wanted to run a football program – and I knew we had to do it my way, win or lose.

✳

Don't be afraid to be wrong. Just remember that even when you're wrong, you're still the boss.

✳

The Protestant reformer Martin Luthur once said, *If you're going to sin, sin boldly.* My translation would read, *If you're going to be wrong, be wrong decisively. Just don't make the same mistake again.*

The fear of making bad decisions has paralyzed many a prospective leader. You'll occasionally see a guy who just sits there nervously twiddling his thumbs until a crisis subsides. The future shapes him. He doesn't shape the future. Another guy, before making a decision, will wet his thumb and hold it up to see how the wind of public opinion is blowing. Either type of leadership is lamentable.

Nothing looks more ridiculous than a leader who is indecisive, uncertain, or reluctant to make difficult decisions. I'd rather be wrong than indecisive. People who perceive fear in their leader may panic themselves. Or lose heart. Or lose respect. They will soon start looking for ways to work around the person in charge. What other choice do they have? A bad leader can bring everyone down.

I watched one coaching staff disintegrate because the head coach was habitually indecisive. This fellow had been a distinguished assistant coach for many years. He was a tough-nosed guy who knew the fundamentals of football. But he carried an assistant coach's mentality into the head coaching job. In his years as an assistant coach, the head coach had always been around to solve problems, make difficult decisions, and bear public scrutiny. Now it was his turn to lead, and he seemed uncomfortable with the responsibility. Part of him still wanted the anonymity and insulation from problems that come with being an assistant.

The way it looked to me, he ignored problems instead of taking charge and facing them head-on. He was unwilling to be the role model that everyone else expected him to be. Well, within a few years his staff was in chaos. Coaches were bickering among themselves. Players were arguing with coaches. No one figured he would do anything about it, and they were correct. The program soon fell to pieces. He and his entire staff were fired after one of the worst losing streaks in school history.

*

Some leaders are too quick to blame others inside the organization for problems they should take responsibility for themselves. To them, *taking charge* means taking the problem out on someone else.

I'll occasionally notice a head football coach who hires and fires his assistant coaches on an almost annual basis. If the defense has a poor year, he fires the defensive coordinator and hires a new coach. If the defense still hasn't improved, he fires the new guy and hires yet another. The head coach appears to be taking charge of a bad situation. I see it differently. My question is, *Why did you hire the guy in the first place if you have to fire him in one or two years? Can't you assess coaching talent any better than that?*

✳

As a leader, you should always be yourself.

Draw insights and lessons from others, but don't try to imitate them, because you aren't them.

Twenty-nine former Bear Bryant assistants went on to become head coaches. Twenty-seven of them got fired. You can learn from a guy like Bryant, but no one can be like him, no matter how hard they try. Each person must be himself.

3
SETTING A PERSONAL EXAMPLE

←──────────────────────→

You're not one of the boys. You are their leader.

Good habits are habit-forming.

Sorry if that sounds redundant, but one of the wisest things a person can do is to practice good habits until the habits become instinctive. Nowhere is this truer than in the arena of leadership. And no habit is more important than the habit of good character.

Good character is a leader's greatest ally. Even if you're young, people will respect the moral principles you stand for.

✳

Character is an action word. We *have* good character only to the extent that we *demonstrate* good character. That's why it's so important for a leader to create good habits. Words are cheap. We are known by our deeds.

✳

People of poor character will get you beat.

Over the course of my career, I've had many opportunities to get involved in business deals. Two of those deals created real problems for me. In both cases, the person who came to me with the deal turned out to be a person of questionable character.

✳

Let me cite two age-old truths that operate like laws of nature. Both truths relate directly to the formation of good character. I hope you learn them the easy way rather than the hard way:

- ✗ Don't say anything you don't want repeated in public, because it probably will be.

- ✗ Don't do anything you don't mind everyone knowing about, because they eventually will know.

Have you ever seen someone get intoxicated and begin disclosing all kinds of things to another colleague? The drunk usually prefaces his disclosure by whispering, *Now don't tell anyone I said this* . . . . Of course, if the revelation is really interesting, it won't be a secret for long. Like the old adage says, the best way for two people to keep a secret is if one of them's dead!

You'd think sober people would exercise better judgment than drunks, but I've seen the same thing happen without alcoholic inducement. If you are the person in charge – and particularly if you are a public figure – your life constitutes interesting conversation for others. They watch you. They enjoy talking about you.

And once the talk begins, it takes on a life of its own.

So be careful about what you say and do. If someone decides to assassinate your character, don't help them by loading the gun.

Some people regard these two age-old truths as a terrible burden. If you're one of those people, then simply accept the burden as the price of leadership. If you wish to lead, you've got to lead by example, which means you've got to set the example.

If you're up to the challenge, then let me repeat myself: First, *don't say anything you don't want repeated in public, because it probably will be*. Don't shoot off at the mouth. Think before you speak. Speak wisely and sincerely. Have other people's best interests at heart. And if you find these things difficult to do, then be humble and try harder. Second, *don't do anything you don't mind everyone knowing about, because they eventually will know*. You're not one of the boys. You are their leader. You must act the part by adhering to a high moral standard.

*

You are the standard-bearer for your organization. Whatever you expect from others, they'd better see it first in you. If you don't want this responsibility, then get out of the way and let someone else carry the flag. Your example will determine whether honesty is important on the job, whether loyalty will be shown to the organization, and whether people will work hard and have a good attitude because they see how important those attributes are to you.

I've never liked the theme some coaches used back in the '40s, '50s, and '60s, which was *Do as I say, not as I do*. I expect from my staff and players only what I'm willing to give myself.

✳

If I curse at my players, the other coaches will be more apt to do it. And if I wink at improprieties, more improprieties will soon follow. If people think that nothing will offend me, I've just opened a Pandora's box of endless problems.

✳

The rhetoric of high moral standards was common stuff back in my youth. I don't mean that people were better then than now. Or worse, either. But we had a deep respect and admiration for people of good character. And we had a clear concept of sin.

We've placed great emphasis these past few decades on the importance of being an open society. I think openness is good. Our society truly is a melting pot of differing customs and ethnic ideologies. But one offshoot of our open society is the almost indiscriminate tolerance of all moral differences and the acceptance of every alternative path on equal terms. We're losing the ability to discriminate between *bad, average, good*, and *better*. It's politically incorrect in some circles to hold people accountable for their bad moral behavior. After all, we might hurt someone's feelings or be thought insensitive if we impose a uniform standard of accountability. Well, let me tell you, giving everyone a trophy regardless of their performance isn't the answer.

Isn't it interesting that we have so few genuine heroes today? Oh, we've got movie action heroes who exterminate the bad guys with a blast from their uzis. And there's no end to popular entertainers who insist upon everyone's freedom of self-expression. But who is left to claim the high moral ground?

Have you also noticed that many modern textbooks on virtue refrain from talking about how we *should* live? They talk instead about *how people once lived* in the past, or *what people once thought*, and *how they live today*. But nothing about how we *should* live. Why? Well, I'm guessing it's because people are afraid they will step on someone's toes if they try to prescribe moral behavior. Mere description is so much easier. Why encourage abstinence when we can pass out condoms and avoid making a value judgment? Why negotiate when we can eliminate disagreements with a gun? Both achieve the same result, don't they?

Hardly.

We've become comfortable with shallow thinking, all the while fancying ourselves to be profound. In effect, we muddy the water to make it look deep.

Give me tough, realistic thinking without sacrificing our historic ideals. *Faith*, *hope*, and *love* are three well-known historic ideals. Leaders once valued them, and prospered. Why aren't they any good anymore?

❋

If you wish to be a leader, then stand for something worth living for. Hold yourself to a high standard. If people perceive your commitment to noble ideals is more important than either of you, they will follow the direction you are headed.

That's one of the great lessons I've learned in 50 years of coaching. No matter how mundane your task, or how irrelevant your work may seem, set a high standard for yourself and resolve to rise above mediocrity.

Allow me to sermonize for one more moment, then I will be quiet on the subject.

When we read about the crucifixion of Jesus, we learn that he was placed between two thieves. All three men ended up dying that day. Two of them died because they fell below the standards of the community. One of them died for rising above it. Society couldn't tolerate either end of the moral spectrum. That tells us a lot about the power of mediocrity. It's difficult to stand for something important.

I've lived through seven decades. I was a child during the Great Depression. I lived through World War II and the wars in Korea, Vietnam, and the Persian Gulf. I've coached players during the Segregation Era, the Civil Rights Era, the Baby Boomer Era, Generation X, and the current Dot-com Generation. My knowledge of the past 70 years doesn't come from books. And I'm not nostalgic to return to the days of my childhood (I like modern dentistry too much!). But we lost sight of something essential when we lost sight of noble ideals. The yearning for tolerance and accommodation should not leave us so open-minded that our brains fall out.

Forget about success for a moment and think instead about leadership. A leader is someone people look up to. A leader is someone people choose to follow because they believe in him. Such leadership begins with the cultivation of good habits, particularly the habits of good character.

✳

Accept your responsibility as a role model.

One message that I repeat constantly to my players and coaches is that we are *all* role models. Every human being is a role model. It is an inescapable fact of life. You're either a good role model or a bad one. Your example is either helpful or harmful. You improve the lives of others or you diminish them. But a role model you most definitely are.

I want my athletes to realize that young people look up to them . . . maybe even idolize them. I tell my players, *Some twelve-year-old boy back in the neighborhood wants to be just like you. Maybe he's having a tough time at home, or he's not doing well in school. Or maybe some other boys in the neighborhood are trying to corrupt him. But he knows about you and thinks you're great. He's decided to make you his role model. So what will he be like if he tries to be just like you?*

Charlie Ward was one of the best role models we've had among our players at FSU. He won the Heisman Trophy in 1993 and was drafted by the New York Knicks to play professional basketball. The Knicks had a reputation for being rough, tough, nasty players. Charlie, on the other hand, had a quiet, gracious demeanor and was a dedicated Christian. It didn't appear that he would fit in. He was certainly in for a rough time. But notice today that at the end of a Knicks game, Charlie and other teammates bow together in prayer, win or lose. Whether you're a religious person or not, you've got to admire that type of influence. Charlie accepts his responsibility as a role model. Guys like that have credibility.

If you want a stark contrast to guys like Charlie, think about some of the high-profile universities whose reputations have been tarnished by coaches of poor character. Some of those schools landed on serious NCAA probation. The coaches themselves either moved on, retired, or got fired. When you're a leader, people are watching. It may be true that you can get away with a lot of stuff if you happen to be successful. The public is quite tolerant of individuals who succeed in acquiring wealth or fame or power. But most people of poor character eventually crash and burn.

✴

Be disciplined in your habits.

It takes discipline to be a good role model. There aren't any shortcuts. If you expect honesty from your staff, you must strive for honesty in your own dealings. If you expect fair play, play fairly. Be the person you expect others to be. Good character is hammered out on the anvil of self-discipline.

Would you like a surefire formula for chaos at work?

Try this one: Find excuses to forgive your own poor performance, then hold others to a different standard. Criticize your colleagues behind their backs. Promise to keep a conversation in confidence, then fail to do so. Sleep with a coworker's spouse. Wink when someone achieves a desired end by undesirable means. And after a while, you will reap what you sow. People won't find you credible. You may still be their boss, but you're not their leader.

Lessons on the value of discipline are easily found in the sports world. Let me tell you a true story about two brothers who played for me at FSU. Their names are Louie and Edgar Richardson. Both boys had great character. And their character showed itself in the form of personal discipline, determination, and persistence.

In 1977, my second year at Florida State, Louie was a fifth-year senior. A 6'5", 225-pound defensive tackle, he had the size to play for us. But he just wasn't good enough. The year before, 1976, we had gone 5-6. A losing season in '77 would really put our fledgling program in a difficult spot. And I just didn't feel that Louie had the talent to play Division I football. So we put him on the scout squad.

Making the scout squad in your senior year is a dead-end road. Nothing is more demoralizing to a senior than to learn he won't play during his last year. But Louie Richardson was a rare breed. Despite his disappointment, he never quit giving his best in practice. He had no chance to play. Yet he went out every practice and tried as hard as he could. The guy just refused to quit on his team.

Being on the scout squad, Louie didn't get to dress out when we played our season opener, which we won. We lost to Miami in our second game. Louie was still wearing street clothes during the game . . . and still watching his teammates from the sidelines. In the third game, our starting defensive tackle went down with an injury. Then our second-string defensive tackle got injured, and we put in our last available replacement. We managed to win the game, but the third-teamer was just too inexperienced to help us. We had no choice but to pull Louie Richardson off the scout squad and make him our starter for the fourth game.

Well, to make a long story short, Louie never lost that starting job – not even after the other two guys got healthy again. Playing like a man possessed, he led us to a 10-2 record and a victory in the Tangerine Bowl in Orlando, Florida. But more remarkably, his effort during those last nine games sparked the attention of professional scouts. Louie Richardson was drafted in the fifth round to play professional football! He ended up having a long career in both the NFL and the Canadian Football League. And he showed us all how good character can lead to a winning program. That 1977 season is perhaps my most satisfying year as a college football coach. In 1979, Louie's younger brother Edgar was our second-team defensive end. We constantly preach to our defenders never to give up on a play. Nothing is more common than to see a defender quit chasing the ball carrier when he sees no chance to tackle him. Young players are most apt to commit this mistake, and Edgar was only a sophomore. Well, we were playing Mississippi State at home that year, and Edgar was in the game helping us protect a six-point lead late in the fourth quarter. Mississippi State lined up in the wishbone and ran an option around the left end. When the ball was snapped, Edgar ran into the backfield only to discover that the play was being run to the other side of the field. And what did he do? He ran around to the other side, and began chasing that quarterback down the field. The quarterback had broken containment on the outside and was running freely downfield. His running back was trailing behind, waiting for a pitch out. And ten yards behind them was Edgar Richardson, running like crazy but gaining no ground. Ten yards . . . 20 yards . . . 40 yards downfield. The quarterback appeared headed for the endzone. And an undefeated season was slipping through our fingers. But here came Edgar, still hustling, still running after that quarterback, and slowly gaining ground. Sure enough, around our 20-yard line, Edgar finally caught up and tackled him from behind. The surprised quarterback fumbled the ball. We recovered it. Edgar's game-saving tackle preserved our lead and our first undefeated regular season at Florida State.

Men like Louie and Edgar Richardson remind me of the importance of determination, persistence, and hard work. Those traits are by-products of good character.

✳

Aim for wisdom.

Wisdom is essential to good leadership, but it doesn't come cheaply. Or quickly.

Most good leaders want wisdom more than any other virtue.

The best leaders seem to have a knack for knowing just what needs to be said in a tense moment. They find solutions that no one else manages to think of. They penetrate to the heart of a problem. And they do things that make bad situations better.

Don't worry if you feel you're not very wise. No one is born wise. But you can learn to be wise. It just takes time . . . and sincere, diligent effort.

No one becomes wise by accident.

Here's what helps me. I try to ask myself, *How could I have handled that situation better? What can I do differently next time that will lead to a more satisfying solution? And have I remained loyal to my deepest convictions?*

✳

No one will ever accuse me of being perfect. But I would be much less of a person – and much less effective as a coach – without a commitment to ideals more valuable than my desire to win.

4
LIVING WITH INTEGRITY

Integrity is all about doing the right thing,
no matter what the consequence.

I wish every problem I faced had an easy solution. But sometimes the right answer to a problem just can't be found in the back of the book. If you've ever raised a child, you know what I mean.

People in the business world deal with ambiguity all the time. Life gets fired at us point-blank. Decisions must be made quickly, sometimes under duress. And we don't have the luxury of saying, *Wait, I need more time. I haven't got it all figured out yet!* We must make the best decisions we can make, then move on to the next issue. Sometimes our decisions are wrong.

That's why integrity is so vital to good leadership.

The leader won't always have time to sort things out. Issues can be fraught with moral ambiguity. Outcomes are not always clear. Yet a decision is demanded NOW. Sometimes the best course isn't clear even if more time is available.

The simplistic response is to say, *Well, a leader should be wise. Wise people will make good decisions in ambiguous situations.*

That's easier said than done. None of us ever becomes perfectly wise. Most of us are never as wise as we need to be. And if you're on the front end of the learning curve, wisdom is what you're hoping for, not something you already have.

So what does one do when wisdom is lacking?

The answer is, ACT WITH INTEGRITY.

When you don't know the answer, the surest course is to do what you believe is right. Follow your conscience. And don't take any action that you believe is morally wrong.

I respect a person who acts with good motives. When someone lives according to high moral principles and acts in the best interests of all concerned, you can't help but admire the person, even when he is wrong. Naturally we expect people to learn from their mistakes. Self-improvement is as much a moral obligation as honesty. But people of integrity aim for the high ground. They may occasionally make bad judgments, but their judgments won't get you in trouble.

MATURITY is the willingness to live with ambiguity.

And INTEGRITY is the answer in the back of the book.

✳

I must demand integrity – from myself and from my staff – if I am to lead successfully. There's no doubt about it. Before I hire anyone, I explain this in the interview.

We run a high-profile program at FSU. People scrutinize everything we do. The slightest chink in the armor will soon be public
knowledge.

I won't be part of a work environment that doesn't put a premium on
integrity. It's not because I'm so good, but because the alternative is
so bad. We've got to play by the rules, run a clean program, and show
genuine love toward one another and toward our athletes. If someone decides they can't make this commitment to integrity, I cannot
afford to keep them on my staff. The consequences for me, my other
coaches, our players, and the university could be disastrous.

I once hired a freshman football coach at West Virginia University.
He was young, single, and very attractive to the women on campus. I found out that after one of our away games, he bought a
case of beer and shared it with some of the female cheerleaders.
When I asked if the rumor was true, he said yes. I then told him
to start looking for another job, because I couldn't retain him
beyond the end of the season.

You cannot be a respected leader if you're willing to compromise your
deepest convictions. I'll rest my case on the strength of this single
assertion: If nothing is kept sacred, all of life soon becomes profane.

*

Many people who lack integrity try to bring others down to their
level. Lacking the discipline to improve themselves, they prefer
that you dishonor yourself.

Your integrity will not make these people comfortable. They

would love to prove you are no better than them. They will tempt and test you. If you give in, you lose.

*

Here's why integrity is so vital to my own success.

1. Landing on NCAA probation will get a coach fired.

I like my job too much to risk getting fired. The folks at FSU will need a crowbar to pry me out of this job.

Anyway, if I got fired for cheating, a new head coach would come in and replace most, if not all, of my assistant coaches with his own people. I cannot let that happen to them as a result of my own misbehavior. I have an obligation to my assistants and their families not to jeopardize their careers. They have the same obligation to me, and I make no bones about it.

Opportunities to cheat are always out there. When you're winning, the temptation isn't all that great because you don't need to cheat. But when the losses start mounting and desperation sets in, the temptation can become almost irresistible.

I can think of at least two head coaches who were not winning and who tried to "pull it out" by buying players. It was too late. Both got caught and lost their jobs. Convicted cheaters carry a tainted reputation for the remainder of their careers. Some are never again offered a head coaching job.

2. I need good morale among my staff if we are to operate effectively. Integrity helps to sustain good morale.

I occasionally make decisions that my coaches don't agree with. Maybe the offensive coaches decide that a wide-open passing attack is our best strategy for the upcoming season, and after listening to their arguments, I veto the proposal. Or perhaps a coordinator's position comes open and three men on my staff want the job. Whomever I select, at least two guys won't like my decision.

In either of these scenarios, my coaches must believe that I'm trying to make the best decision for the program and for all of us as a unit. Otherwise, I'll have to contend with a disgruntled staff.

Coaching staffs tend to do one of two things over time: either they become a unified and cohesive band of brothers, or they begin to fracture and disintegrate. Integrity is the glue that holds the pieces together, and it must begin with the leader.

3. Nothing hurts team unity worse than disingenuousness.

I once worked for a guy who was always afraid that an assistant coach might be jockeying for his job. Let an assistant coach get a nice write-up in the newspaper, or receive praise from the fans, and immediately our boss would assume that some conspiracy was underfoot. He was wrong, of course, but try telling him that! What he did was to start talking about certain assistant coaches behind their backs. He didn't just talk to boosters or to school personnel outside our office. He also talked to other assistant coaches on the staff, telling them, *If old so-and-so thinks he's getting my job, he'd better watch himself.* But then when he presided over our staff meetings, you'd think he loved us all like brothers.

The whole situation left me feeling very uneasy. I mean, for goodness sakes, if he's talking disparagingly about one of my colleagues, what might he be saying about me? Such disingenuousness destroys trust and eats away at morale. I soon began looking for another job. This one wasn't worth the trouble.

At 71 years of age, I know people have already begun talking about my replacement at FSU. Such talk is inevitable. I just don't want it to cause problems on my staff. I still enjoy coaching at FSU. As long as I'm happy and my health is good, I plan to stay here. The men on my staff, however, have a right to know about my plans. So I shoot straight and tell them what they need to know:

Men, I don't plan on retiring any time soon. If my thinking changes, I'll let you know before anyone else, so you can begin making plans.

I know you have to think about the future . . . about what will happen to you after I retire. Whoever replaces me may want to bring in his own coaches and let you go. If your wife is like mine, she won't fail to remind you of this possibility.

Some of you may not want to wait and find out what happens. Maybe you've decided to go ahead and start looking elsewhere for a job. Just know that I don't want you to go. We've created something special here at FSU, and I'll do what I can to keep you. But if you decide to start looking, keep me posted, and I'll help you if you feel it's time to move on.

If you choose to stay, then rest assured I'll keep you abreast of my thinking. If my thinking changes, you'll be the first to know.

In the meantime, men, if I ever discover that someone is jockeying to be my replacement before I'm ready to be replaced, well, I can't keep a person like that on my staff. Some booster or alumnus may come to you with all sorts of ideas about how you fit in after I'm gone. My advice is to ignore them. Don't say anything that might get you hanged.

Men, I'll be honest with you about my plans, because I owe you that. But I won't tolerate disloyalty.

I hold a week-long staff meeting every July, and every July I share my thoughts on retirement, caveats and all. When the meeting is over, we all know where we stand.

4. I prize integrity because it helps me win games.

My players will practice harder, and thereby perform better, if they know we coaches have their best interests at heart. We can't win if the guys in the trenches don't trust what we're asking them to do. And we do expect these boys to trust in our judgment.

Sometimes a great player needs to be shifted to a different position. Warrick Dunn and Deion Sanders were exceptionally gifted high school quarterbacks when we recruited them. Both were asked to play defensive back at Florida State. Dunn was later shifted to running back. Both players became All-Americans at their new positions.

Players aren't always eager to make these changes. Some of them have professional football in their long-range plans. If a guy thinks he can be drafted as a quarterback, why should he move to a new position that he hasn't played before?

Dan Kendra, whose father played for me at West Virginia, was one of these players. Voted the number-one high school quarterback in America after his senior season, he signed with FSU in 1995 and sat patiently through a redshirt freshman year. By his sophomore year, he advanced to second-team quarterback and had greatness written all over him.

Dan was an amazing physical specimen. As a 6'2", 240-pound freshman, he set the weight room record among all of our players with a leg press of 1335 pounds! He bench-pressed over 500 pounds. This kid was chiseled from head to toe, and he ran the 40-yard dash in 4.55 seconds. Had he not wanted to play quarterback, he probably could've started as a sophomore at linebacker, tight end, or fullback. But it takes three years in our system before a quarterback is experienced enough to run the offense.

Dan finally got his opportunity to shine after the '97 season. He was slated as our starting quarterback when we entered spring ball in 1998. Then tragedy struck. He tore up his knee on the last day of spring practice and needed surgery to repair torn ligaments. His doctor advised him to rehab the knee for one year, which meant he would have to sit out the entire '98 fall football season. Still, he could come back in '99 for his senior year and one last shot at impressing the professional scouts.

With Kendra out of the line-up, we had to start the '98 season with our second-string quarterback – a 26-year-old codger named Chris Weinke, who took us to the national championship game against Tennessee.

When Dan came back for the 1999 season, Weinke was firmly entrenched as our starting quarterback. Weinke ended up taking us to three straight national championship games – one of which we won in 1999 – and he won the Heisman Trophy after the 2000 season.

And here's Dan Kendra, Mr. All-Everything in high school and one of the most excitable and dedicated players I've coached, who wouldn't even get to play quarterback during his senior year in '99.

Dan came to me and asked if he could move to fullback. I thought that was a great idea. Even though he had never played the position and had not learned the blocking assignments and techniques, we thought he might have a career beyond college at the fullback slot. That or linebacker, for which he was even less prepared. The techniques and coverages required of linebackers were too much for him to learn in one season. We owed him a shot at something and felt he would be excellent at fullback.

Anyway, Dan made the move and did a good job for us. The Baltimore Ravens were impressed enough that they signed him to a professional contract as a fullback.

I do not go up to a player and simply inform him, *We've decided that you will play a different position.* No way would I do that to a player today. He might walk off the team. Rather, his position coach or I will say, *Son, we need depth at cornerback, and here are the reasons we think you might want to play that position. . . . Give it your best thought and let me know by the end of the week.* If he is opposed to the move, we'll leave him where he is. It's not right to tell a recruit that he can play quarterback, and then force him into a new position once he arrives on campus. Future recruits wouldn't trust us. We cannot win without trust.

※

Integrity makes my job easier. It's deception and dishonesty that require so much diligent effort.

If you lie to people, you must constantly try to remember which lies you told to whom. Keeping track of all the lies is hard work. And if someone finds out you've been dishonest, at the very least you'll lose the authority that comes with credibility.

When I think of liars, I think of the gambler who loses five dollars and then bets another five to get even. After losing a second time, he puts down 10 to get even, then 20, then 40, but he continues to lose. After a while his entire bankroll is gone and he thinks to himself, *Gee, if I'd only not gambled in the first place, I'd still have all my money.* Lying works a lot like gambling. You need lies to cover your lies. And every lie is a losing hand.

Honesty is so much easier.

✹

In my life, integrity and religious faith are inseparably related. My one great source of strength is faith in God. Faith doesn't make me perfect, but it sure points me in the right direction. I don't worry as much about what other people think, because I believe God has a plan for my life. God's plan may not be my plan, but I try to trust Him and press ahead.

5

LOYALTY

←————————————————————————→

When loyalty is thrown to the wind,
it creates a whirlwind of trouble.

The first chink in the armor of any organization is usually disloyalty.

✳

The word LOYALTY appears on the first page of my hideaway notes. In fact, among the various items listed on that first page, loyalty is right at the top, along with the following statement:

We will be loyal to one another – I will defend you, and you will have to defend me. It starts there with loyalty.

Why?

Because of adversity.

Adversity will come, and when it does, it will work to divide us, to pit one man against another, and weaken the unity so necessary to success.

I cannot allow disunity.

✳

To create loyalty among my staff, the first thing I do is *demand* it.

In the interview process, I tell a prospective new coach that loyalty is a necessity. I will not keep a disloyal coach on my staff.

I make sure everyone knows my feelings on the subject.

The second thing I do is *practice* it.

✳

My belief is that you should always defend your staff until or unless the facts mandate otherwise. Wait until all the facts are in before withholding support of anyone. You hurt your credibility if you prematurely jump to a conclusion and then are proved wrong.

✳

Most coaches learn that during times of adversity, you circle the wagons and remain loyal to one another. If you've never had your company's performance scrutinized by the media on a daily basis, or had the least little mishap broadcast nationwide, it may take you longer to learn this lesson.

We coaches learn rather quickly that we succeed or fail together. If we don't support one another, we all may end up losers.

*

The most memorable act of loyalty I know about in the coaching profession occurred several years ago at a university in the southeast.

An athletic director telephoned his head coach one morning and asked for a meeting. The season had gone poorly, the A.D. explained, and changes would need to be made. Two assistant coaches were singled out for blame. By innuendo, the coach was being told to fire them.

Upon leaving the A.D.'s office, the head coach called his staff together to explain the situation. He disagreed with the A.D.'s assessment and said that firing two coaches would be wrong. Yet going against the A.D.'s instructions might cause even worse problems. The meeting became quietly intense as each man pondered his future.

Then the head coach shared his decision. From his point of view, every coach had done what was asked of him. No assistant had been derelict in his duty or disloyal to his superiors. Consequently, no one would be fired. They would stick together and aim for a better record next year.

This particular head coach is a friend of mine. I know he's a good, solid coach. And I suspect the A.D. hated that meeting as much as he did. I won't make an excuse for either of them. But as a fellow coach, I understand what must've been going through the minds of all those men in the room. They knew full well that wins and losses aren't always under a coach's control.

Goodness, look at Mike Krzyzewski's experience at Duke during his first three years. He lost more basketball games than he won!

I'm sure there were fans and alumni who figured he couldn't win at Duke. I can write the script: *Gee, just look at his losing record. And look at what Dean Smith is accomplishing up the road at North Carolina. There's just too much money at stake for us to sit by idly. We can't win with this Krzyzewski fellow.*

Imagine if the school had given up on him after his third year. Duke University may not have won three national championships.

We coaches understand that not every problem is attributable to bad coaching.

Injuries to a few key players, for example, can mean the difference between winning and losing. Think about an injury to your starting center. When you lose him, you've lost the one player who calls out blocking assignments for the other linemen on each play. When the center lines up over the ball at the start of each play, he glances up to read the defensive alignment. It takes a lot of experience to do that well. The same holds true for the quarterback, who must read the defensive secondary and change the play if necessary. Once the center recognizes the alignment, he barks out a code word or makes a gesture indicating how the rest of the offensive line is to block – maybe zone blocking, or slant blocking. But what happens if your center gets injured and must leave the game?

Well, you go to your number-two center. This guy obviously is not quite as good as the guy he's replacing, or else he'd be starting himself. And he obviously hasn't had as much work with the first-team linemen during weekly practice. So he's not as familiar with the particular defensive alignments that the opponent may show him.

You can get by with a second-team center, but you also can count on some missed assignments and busted plays. And if – God forbid! –

the second-teamer is an inexperienced freshman or sophomore who isn't sure about his own blocking assignments, much less everyone else's, it's likely to be even worse. Maybe the coach tries to mitigate this dilemma by moving the All-American tackle over to the guard position where he can help out. But then you've got to put someone at that tackle position. This is what I call *the game within the game.* Shift players around. Shore up weaknesses. And improvise with the material that's available.

Coaches play these chess matches every Saturday. Untimely injuries can ruin a well-conceived game plan.

Let one receiver run a wrong route, or one lineman block the wrong defender, and a play is ruined. Let it happen too often, and a game is ruined. Lose some key players to injury, and a season is ruined. My coaching colleagues know this only too well.

When the staff meeting ended, the head coach returned to the A.D.'s office and refused to fire any of his assistants. He offered his rationale and then left.

Several days later, the head coach and his entire staff were dismissed.

In retrospect, you may say the coach made a dumb decision. Instead of two men losing their jobs, they all got fired. Where's the virtue in that? Well, maybe it was dumb, maybe it wasn't. Who knows what would've happened to them after the next football season?

But I'll tell you this. I know nine men today who will walk through fire for their former head coach. Whether he was smart or dumb as measured by career success, he refused to fire innocent coaches simply to please others. And he can count on a letter of highest recommendation from me any time he asks for it.

People will rally around a leader who is loyal to them. So will players.

✳

I once read in the newspaper about an assistant coach who took a tape recorder with him into a staff meeting – something he had never done before.

According to accounts, he had secretly been told that the head coach would soon be forced to resign, and that he, the assistant, would become the new head coach. But first some evidence was needed to justify the head coach's ouster. Perhaps an unguarded statement by the head coach could be captured on tape during a staff meeting. Such seems to have been the plan. Unfortunately for the folks behind the scenes, the tape recording episode was a bust. No incriminating information was forthcoming.

This situation had disaster written all over it, as so often happens when disloyalty and dishonesty prevail. The head coach did resign under pressure, but someone from another school was brought in as his replacement. The assistant coach resigned in anger over the deception. Then he sued the university and related personnel, alleging that he had been duped with lies. It was an expensive, embarrassing affair.

When loyalty is thrown to the wind, it creates a whirlwind of trouble.

✳

I've got a reputation among a few of our alumni as an indulgent coach who will keep bad players rather than booting them from the team. Some folks think I tend to look the other way. I don't. But I am unapologetically loyal to my players, as much as I can be. It's something I owe to my players and their parents.

Loyalty doesn't mean I shy away from discipline. But it does mean I don't ask outsiders how I should handle my business.

When a negative story comes out in the press citing bad behavior by one of our players, I can count on receiving mail from one or two distraught alums. The letters usually begin like this:

Dear Coach Bowden,

Up until recently, I have been a proud alumnus of Florida State University. But when I read about one of your players getting into trouble, only to find that you haven't kicked him off the team, I am embarrassed to be associated with the school any longer. Your lack of integrity, and your win-at-all-costs mentality, are dragging the name of a fine institution through the mud.

I once read all of my mail. Now I throw these letters away the minute I see what they are. I don't resent the authors. They just lack a good grasp on the facts.

I did write back to one indignant alum, however, with the following message:

Dear _____ ,

If your child came to FSU and got into trouble, would you prefer that I assist your child in whatever way I can until you arrive, or would you rather I join the mob who wants him lynched?

I have influence either way.

Please advise.

I never heard back from the guy, which is why I normally don't bother to read such letters.

I try to treat my players the same way I treated my children when they were young. You discipline your kids, but you don't throw them to the wolves. Players are dismissed from the team if they violate university guidelines or fail my "three strikes" test. Otherwise, they are disciplined internally – out of the public eye – according to policies established by the coaches.

Which option is in a player's best interest: to keep him on the team, discipline him, and continue to monitor him, or to throw him on the street and wash your hands of him? Don't forget, some of these boys come from broken homes, poor families, and rough neighborhoods. Many have never had a male role model, no one to insist that they make decent grades, no one to get in their face and discipline them, and no one to give them a sense of direction.

I remind myself that every player's mother is hoping I'll take care of her son while he's here at Florida State. If you love your children, you discipline them but you don't throw them out of the house when they make mistakes, not even big mistakes, if you can help it. Why people want us coaches to do less with our players is beyond me.

Let me tell you the story of Todd Williams, who currently plays football at a university in the southeast. You can watch him play this fall on TV.

Todd's childhood was an extended story of tragedy and hardship.

His father rejected him at birth, refusing to sign his birth certificate at the hospital when Todd was born. His mother was unable to care for him, so he went to live with his grandmother, who took care of him until the day she died. But her death came too early. Todd was only 13 years old.

He went to Texas and lived with some relatives there, but that didn't work out. Then he moved in with relatives in Miami, but that didn't work out either. Todd had no desire to be someone's foster child. So he came back to Bradenton, Florida, and lived on his own. He made his home in an abandoned building and did whatever he needed to feed himself.

Todd had great size and athletic ability. At 6'5" and 300 pounds, he was a boy in a man's body. And yet he was a boy without a home.

He enrolled in high school and tried out for the football team. It was the high school coach who first came to Todd's aid. The coach invited Todd to live with him until a better solution could be found. Then a local minister got involved. The minister's congregation raised enough money to get Todd a place to live. Then they found him a job. The football coach and the minister were the only two authority figures in Todd's life.

The past, however, is not always easy to overcome. Bitterness, resentment, and bad habits may still linger. Indeed, Todd got into trouble during his senior year, and the football coach suspended him for a few ballgames. College recruiters began backing away, despite Todd's great size and athletic ability, because they feared the obstacles were just too great for him to overcome.

Some schools remained interested, however, and Todd eventually accepted a scholarship to play college football. Almost three years have passed since that day. Against imposing odds, he has stayed the course and made a name for himself. And when the fall season begins, he will line up at the starting offensive tackle spot . . .

Wearing jersey #79 . . .

At Florida State!

I'm glad we got Todd. He has surpassed all our expectations. Few people I know could survive his ordeal. The next time some national media outlet wants to run a story on a college football player, I wish they'd tell Todd's story.

Here's a kid who was raised next door to disaster. He had no family. No support group. No money. No one big enough or brave enough to get in his face. And no chance. But a coach, a minister, and a church stepped in. Then he goes off to college and encounters coaches who impose rules, bark out instructions, and push him hard to become better than he already is. Those same coaches wonder, *Will he rebel against authority? Will he quit and walk away?* No, he doesn't rebel. He does just the opposite. He works hard. He goes to class. He keeps his nose clean.

And now he's a starter here at Florida State.

Were there difficult moments? *Of course.* Did he get discouraged and want to quit? *Sure he did.* But he stuck with it, and we'll stick with him.

Much of my loyalty to players owes to the difficulties some of them have faced in life. They come to Florida State and live under more public scrutiny than most people can imagine. Because of our high public profile, they are one bad judgment away from having their faces plastered all over the sports page by some writer eager for an incriminating story about athletes. These kids don't need a tyrant threatening to throw them back on the street. They need a father. My staff and I try to fill that role as best we can.

Loyalty is the starting point.

※

How important is loyalty to good leadership?

Try running an organization where you are loyal to no one, and no one is loyal to you. Then call me six months later and tell me how things are going.

6
HUMILITY

←——————————————————————→

Humility is wisdom's prerequisite.

None of us takes easily to humility. We don't like being humbled by life. We'd rather pay a different price for life's lessons.

But humbled we become. And humiliation comes most often at our own hands. If we are honest enough to admit our errors and learn from them, we have a chance to become wise.

✳

Overconfidence has never been my strong suit. I've always been driven to win by the fear of failure. Now, don't get me wrong. I am a competitive person. I coach football for the same reason I played it as a young man – I want to excel and beat the other guy. My greatest pleasure as a coach is to develop strategies and construct game plans. I want to match wits with the guy across the field. But I hate losing more than I like winning. Losing poses the threat that maybe, just maybe, I don't measure up.

I cannot speak for Coach Steve Spurrier at Florida, but I believe he and I are opposites in self-motivation. I prepare extensively because of my fear of losing. I could be wrong, but I believe Steve's motivation is his confidence in winning.

I admire coaches who believe in themselves and are quietly confident in their abilities. I like to measure myself against them on the field. Many great leaders have this quality of quiet self-confidence. Many of my players have that quality, too. But one step away from self-confidence is another set of traits that can bring a person down in a hurry: overconfidence, brashness, and arrogance.

✳

Many leaders, especially if they enjoy a measure of public notoriety, must wrestle seriously with the issue of humility. The more successful one is, the more accolades one receives. And the temptation becomes great to forget that you could ever do anything wrong. You know you're fallible, but you hate to admit it.

I mean, c'mon, everyone says you're great. Can so many people be wrong?

Yep.

Some younger leaders think they must consistently project an image of strength and unwavering self-confidence. They see humility as a sign of weakness. I see it differently. I think humility is a sign of honesty.

I've found that the higher up you go in an organization, from vice presidents to presidents to CEOs to chairmen of the board, the more humility you tend to find. This isn't always true, but it's true in most instances.

Humble people can still be confident in their abilities. They can still be courageous in difficult moments. But they're not tempted to play God or act pretentiously.

＊

I don't need to believe in humility. All I need is a good memory. Lord knows, I've made my share of bad decisions and poor judgments during the past 50 years in coaching.

I recall my earliest days at South Georgia College in Douglas, Georgia. I was a 26-year-old head football coach, and we had this guy on our team who was two years older than me. He was a man's man, no doubt about it. A full-blooded Cherokee Indian: 28 years old, 6'5" tall, 260 pounds. That was big for a football player back in the 1950s. The other players called him Big Jim.

Now Big Jim had a real good nose for trouble. And if he couldn't find some, he'd create it. He was always getting into trouble. Only we didn't know it at first.

He transferred to South Georgia College after "messing up" at Florida State. Of course, in those days, we gave a uniform to anyone who could play a lick. This guy wore an extra large. We were more than happy to have him on our junior college team.

But our happiness was short-lived. Several weeks after his arrival on campus, I received a call from the local sheriff. It seems Big Jim had caused a ruckus in town and gotten arrested. While incarcerated that evening, he tried to burn down the jail – with him in it! The sheriff called me after the smoke cleared. We got Big Jim squared away back on campus, and I imposed a strenuous disciplinary regimen that would help to reform his bad judgment.

I also sat him down in the following days and explained that he should live as an example for others to follow. My speech ended with the admonition that if he chose to cause any more trouble, he better leave town and do it in the next county.

I wasn't seriously suggesting that he actually cause trouble in the next county, which I assumed he understood. I just wanted to emphasize that he should be a role model in our local community.

Well, so much for assumptions. I received a call the following weekend from the sheriff in the adjoining county. Big Jim was in jail over in Ocilla, Georgia. This time it was a barroom brawl, and he'd given a pretty bad beating to the sheriff's deputies when they showed up to restore law and order. Thank goodness I was coaching at a junior college and not a major university. Otherwise, this would have been front-page news.

I tried everything I knew to get Big Jim's life turned around, including counseling him and taking him to church with my family. But my best efforts failed. He tried hard to improve his behavior. He even showed his dedication at practice one day by announcing that I should hit him on the chin, right there in front of all the other players, as recompense for disobeying me! He really did try to improve. But try as he might, he simply couldn't reform himself. Other incidents occurred. One fight involved knives. Worries began to crop up about his mental stability. Would he attack some of our players, or even us coaches? I wish I had been wise enough to help him, but I wasn't.

What I finally did was to visit him in his dorm room one day and tell him a lie. I told him that the University of Southern Mississippi in Hattiesburg had a football scholarship for him, and that he should head that way immediately. So he packed his bags and hitchhiked that evening all the way to Hattiesburg, Mississippi.

Meanwhile, I advised the local sheriff not to allow him back into our county. Then I called the head coach at Southern Mississippi to tell him a big, brawny recruit had been sent his way. That's when I learned that Southern Miss was out of scholarships.

Once in Hattiesburg, Big Jim discovered my deception. There was no scholarship waiting for him. There was no new beginning. Two days later he called me and asked why I lied.

I had some sleepless nights following that phone call. What I did wasn't right. In fact, it was downright yellow. I had abandoned a player instead of trying to help him. I resolved not to do that again. To this day, I'll defend my players and support them unless circumstances prohibit me from doing so. I believe their parents would hope for as much from me.

✳

As if personal failures aren't enough to keep me humble, my job adds all the additional humility I need.

My worst coaching nightmare dates back to 1970, my first year as a Division I head coach. My West Virginia team was playing Pittsburgh on their home field. To West Virginians, the WVU-Pitt game is every bit as important as the Alabama-Auburn, Ohio State-Michigan, or USC-UCLA rivalries. And, oh man, this one couldn't have started any better. By halftime, we were ahead 35-6. It was shaping up to be a blowout, and I was feeling pretty good down there on the sidelines. Sunday's headlines would be sweet: FIRST-YEAR HEAD COACH PROVES TOO MUCH FOR HIS MAIN RIVAL.

The Pitt fans had given up. Most of them left the stadium at half-time. Those who stayed were subject to merciless jeers by some of the West Virginia fans. It was ugly. Still, this would be a victory for me and my staff to savor. So I decided to play conservatively in the final two quarters and not do anything to get us beat. Up 35-6, why do anything else?

Then the impossible began to unfold. Pitt decided to run the ball every down in the second half, even on fourth down. They slowly ground out first downs and kept the ball out of our hands. Meanwhile, their defense stiffened and shut down my conservative efforts not to lose. We didn't score another point.

By the time the final gun sounded, we had lost the game 36-35!

State police had to escort me from the locker room to the team bus for the drive home. I thought those West Virginia fans were going to kill me. I think some wanted to. Bobby Bowden was not the success he hoped to be. He was a failure. Or so it seemed at the time.

People who wonder why I require a big lead before I call off the dogs weren't with me in West Virginia after the Pitt game. A half-time lead of 35-6 does *not* make me comfortable.

I also learned not to get away from doing what works. My first-half strategy was riskier, but it's the strategy we opted for after watching weeks of film on Pitt's defense. Getting away from it cost me the game.

❋

I've learned not to rush to judgment when someone else proves fallible just like me. Humbling experiences have enabled me to become more supportive of those around me.

I think one major reason our players push themselves harder than players at many other schools is because they know their coaches care for them and support them. The men on my staff have the same attitude when dealing with one another. A healthy dose of humility goes a long way toward creating an atmosphere of mutual support, trust, loyalty, and high morale.

❋

Humility has also enabled me to better guard against my own weaknesses. When you are painfully aware of your own weaknesses, you learn to consciously work around them. So you're less vulnerable to having those weaknesses exploited by an opponent.

❋

The opposite of humility is arrogance.

I don't mind going head-to-head with an arrogant adversary on the football field, because chances are he is blind to some of his weaknesses. He's so good he doesn't think he has weaknesses. That's fine with me. I'll just be looking that much closer to discover and exploit his blind spot.

Sometimes you don't even have to exploit it, because they do it for you.

I recall a game we played back in the early 1990s. We had an All-American receiver named Tamarick Vanover who also returned punts for us. I think he led the nation in punt returns that year and had a number of returns for touchdowns. He had both size and speed.

Now if it had been me, I would've kicked short every time in order to keep the ball out of Tamarick's hands. But our opponent that day was ranked higher than we were, and the coach must've assumed that Tamarick was not really that big a threat. They kicked off deep, and Tamarick returned that kickoff over 80 yards for a touchdown. On their next kickoff, they kicked deep again, and this time Tamarick returned it for a 75-yard touchdown. On their third kickoff, one of their players made a shoestring tackle to prevent yet a third touchdown. Then they quit kicking off to him. Tamarick got us 14 points in two plays.

We won the game.

✳

Humility has taught me to be open to new ideas and new ways to improve, both as a person and as a coach. I've proven how dumb I can be at times. It's made me more interested in the ideas of others.

I encourage my staff to think independently of me and to argue for their alternative points of view. What a shame if I refused to draw readily on their experience or refused to benefit from their insights. One of the biggest problems with an arrogant person is that there's nothing others can teach him. Why should he listen to his staff or employees when he already knows it all? What a waste of the creative insights and good common sense that others possess. And what better way to miss golden opportunities to make improvements.

*

Humility is not a virtue that any of us enjoys learning. We'd rather have the wisdom to avoid life's humiliations. Or maybe the courage to rise above them. We'd rather have any virtue other than humility, because humility comes only at the cost of personal failure. But fail we will, and not just once or twice.

Maybe wisdom, in its essence, is good judgment learned through failures unforgotten yet unrepeated.

*

Humility and honesty go hand in hand. What is humility if not an honest appraisal of one's own fallibility? And what is arrogance if not dishonesty to oneself? If a guy can't even be honest with himself, I'm not sure you want to follow his lead.

*

Look again at the truly great leaders in human history, both men and women. They all walk with a limp. They carry their failures with them.

7
WORK HABITS

*My code has always been to work like this is the last job I'll ever have,
and live like it's the last day of my life.*

Folks who warn about the "workaholic mentality" will be unhappy with what I say here. I've always worked long hours. And my habits won't change unless I retire or my health deteriorates. You cannot be successful in this business if you're unwilling to work long hours.

During the regular football season, my coaches and I have six days to prepare for the next ballgame. Let's say that we just played Clemson on Saturday night, and Miami is coming to town the following Saturday. Our preparation for the Miami game will begin on Sunday morning after the Clemson game. Though I don't require it, my coaches may be in the office as early as 7 A.M., watching game film on Miami and developing a game plan. We must have our basic plan worked out before the players report for practice on Monday afternoon. Any new plays we want to put in, or new alignments or blocking schemes we'll use, or whatever tendencies Miami has that our players need to be aware of, all must be resolved at the first of the week. The offensive coaches meet together, watch film, discuss strategies, and then watch more film until they feel confident about how we should attack our opponent. The defensive coaches do the same.

My day begins between 4:30 and 5:00 A.M. On Monday through Friday, I'm in the office between 6 and 7 A.M. The staff meeting begins at 8:30, then we all watch more film until practice at 3:30 P.M. After practice, the offensive and defensive coaches will meet again to evaluate the day's practice, watch more film, and discuss strategy. They may not get home until 11 P.M.

In my younger years, I was the first to arrive and the last to leave. These days, I head home around 6:30 P.M. and take my wife to dinner. When we get back home, I go to my room, shut the door, and watch film until around midnight. These are routine hours for coaches on Monday through Thursday during the football season.

Friday's schedule is about the same, except that our players and coaches are bused about 30 miles out of town that afternoon to a hotel in Thomasville, Georgia. We do this to ensure that everyone's attention remains focused on the next day's game. We'll check into our rooms, share a meal together, and then the coaches and players meet until around 9:30 P.M. Once these meetings break up, I meet with my offensive staff until maybe midnight, going over down-and-distance scenarios and ensuring that we've got the right plays in the playbook for this game.

On Saturday, we bus back to Tallahassee about four hours before the game. The coaches will continue to meet together, review film, and go over assignments with the players. Then we play the game. A night game might end at 10 P.M. When the final gun sounds, I go immediately to meet with the press, an endeavour that may last

20-40 minutes. Then I'm escorted off to a broadcast studio where I spend 30 minutes doing our post-game radio show. Afterwards, I'll shower and head off to tape the weekly TV show that we broadcast every Sunday for our fans. I'm home by 1 A.M. and up again at 5 A.M. On Sunday morning I read the newspaper, then head off to an 8 A.M. breakfast meeting with the news media at a local Tallahassee hotel, which gets me back home around 11 A.M. Once I'm home, I'll nap for a little while, then the weekly routine begins again.

In my situation, leadership requires me to work however long it takes to get the job done. If I wanted an eight-to-five job, I'd have to look somewhere other than coaching.

*

I cannot do much to lessen the hectic pace of my schedule. But I've learned to rest whenever and wherever I can.

During the week, I take "power naps" that help to sustain me. I tell my secretary not to disturb me between 1 and 2 P.M. That's my nap time. I'll kick my shoes off, prop my bare feet on the corner of the desk, and lean back into a comfortable angle of repose. The nap may last anywhere from 15 to 50 minutes, but when I awaken, I'm fresh and ready to go.

I sleep better when traveling than I do in bed. A two-hour plane trip means one hour and 45 minutes of sleep. In a car or bus, I'll nap for 10 minutes if the drive lasts that long.

I once laid down and fell asleep on a locker-room bench waiting for our game to start against Miami. One of the players woke me up. He was afraid I might miss the kickoff.

✳

Despite my work habits, I do not believe that long hours in the office guarantee success.

I can name a couple of current head football coaches who demand excessively long hours from their assistant coaches. One new head coach called his staff together and told them they could each have two weekends off over the next twelve months!

I'd rather not work for a guy like that. But I've been in equally difficult circumstances.

Goodness, I once worked for a head coach who never liked being alone at the office. He wanted everyone else there just in case he thought of something to discuss with the rest of us. So if he chose to go into the office at 6 A.M. on Sunday morning, he called all of us assistants and told us to get in there. If he decided to head back to the office at 10 P.M., we got the call to meet him there. He simply expected us to show up whenever he showed up. I didn't like that, and I will not treat my staff that way.

I ask my coaches to get their jobs done. They know what's at stake if we start losing ballgames. But if they work efficiently and get their jobs done with time to spare, that's great. And if they want to go to church with their families on Sunday mornings during the football season, I won't do anything to alter those plans. In fact, I don't hold Sunday staff meetings because I want church time kept open.

I just want the work done when we need it done.

✳

Average coaches lack personal discipline and work habits. Nothing is more common than unsuccessful men with talent.

✳

One of the great lessons I've learned in 50 years of coaching is to delegate responsibilities to my staff.

There was a time when I felt the need to oversee every little thing my staff did. It wasn't that I didn't trust them to do their jobs. I just took my head coaching job very seriously, and I felt obligated to stay on top of everything that was going on.

Even into my 40s, while I was the head coach at WVU, I would often stay at the office until midnight during the football season. I watched film endlessly. I met with defensive coaches and with offensive coaches and reviewed every detail of our game plan. I met with every player who had a problem. My fear was that if I didn't stay on top of things, we might lose football games.

I do a lot of delegating now. It's better that way. I trust my staff to do their jobs, and they enjoy having both the added responsibility and the added authority. We win more games when I leave them alone to do what they do best. It gets back to having staff members you can trust to do what is expected of them.

Of course, I will watch the younger coaches more closely to ensure that they're staying on top of things.

*

Because of the long hours that coaching demands, I've always looked for ways to blend family life with work.

When I was at Samford University back in the early 1960s, I often took my three oldest sons with me to away games and on recruiting trips. All three children were still quite young. And they loved making those away-game trips with the players.

We drove a team bus to away games. Our college bus was typical of buses in those days, with straight-back vinyl seats and a long, silver metal luggage rack overhead. After the game, on the ride back from Mississippi or Tennessee, my sons would get sleepy. We took football jerseys and made pallets up there on that luggage rack. Fortunately, none of them ever rolled out of bed. I guess putting my kids up there was a dangerous thing to do. A person who did that today would probably get arrested for wanton endangerment, but we didn't think of it that way back then. Anyway, modern buses have those little fiberglass luggage compartments with the snap-shut doors. The kids wouldn't fit.

I did look for ways to get my children around me. Oftentimes I took one of them with me to a speaking engagement or a golf outing. Up until the time they were grown and gone, each of my sons made recruiting trips with me, and I'll tell you, it's not a lonely drive when you take your boys along. Even in my earliest years at South Georgia College back in the late 1950s, when I was also a lifeguard at the college swimming pool during the summer months, my wife and children often came over for a day at the pool.

My two daughters never made any of the recruiting trips, but I did take them to speaking engagements. The engagements often gave me four to eight quality hours with them. I did this with each girl until she was around 15 years old. At that age, they found more interesting things to do than take trips with their old man.

For the past 50 years, I have vacationed for two weeks each June with my wife and children at the beach in Florida. Along the way, we've added 21 grandchildren to the roster. Work has never been allowed to interfere with our family vacation time. I don't even call into the office to check messages. As amazing as it may sound, the world works fine without me.

✳

Emerson once said that materialism is in the saddle, and it rides us.

His point is that we must constantly be on the vigil to ensure that the things we own don't eventually come to own us.

Modern technology is a case in point. With faxes, e-mail, and cellular phones, we can work from just about any locale – from the office, at home, in a different country, on the golf course, in a restaurant, or even while traveling. Such convenience is one of the virtues of modern technology.

But too much of a virtue becomes a vice.

We must not allow work to dominate, or intrude into, every waking moment of our lives.

I've just now begun to carry a mobile phone with me when away from the office. I don't know my cellular number, and I don't turn the phone on unless my secretary says she'll need to call me.

Technology is nice, but I don't want work chasing me everywhere I go.

✹

Everyone needs some private place they go to escape the pressures of life. Golf is my escape. I play golf from March until the end of June each year. Count on me being at the practice range or the golf course every free minute I have. My secretary knows to tell callers that "He's out until three o'clock today" or "He's out looking at real estate." Golf is the one hobby that gets my mind off coaching.

Come July, I put the clubs away and don't touch them again until the following March. Football is all I want to think about when July rolls around.

8
TIME MANAGEMENT

←————————————————————→

Anybody can coach a three-hour practice.
A great coach can organize it in one and one-half hours.

Success is often the biggest threat to continued success.

Why?

Because the more successful you are, the more in demand you become. This is especially true in a high-profile career like college coaching. And as your schedule fills up with extracurricular activities, you have less time to do the one thing that made you successful in the first place.

It's a dangerous irony of success.

Your own day planner may be crowded with references to committee meetings, civic luncheons, professional conferences, board meetings, charitable functions, public speeches, and so forth — all of which you do as the leader of your organization. My schedule is filled with some of these same functions, along with recruiting visits, booster meetings, fund raisers, media interviews, TV appearances, and various promotional events.

Let me give you a sampling of my annual January-May schedule. It's a typical routine for any major college football coach. We learn in a hurry that if our time is not managed carefully, our football programs may soon become models of inefficiency and chaos.

Every winter I make recruiting visits between early January and early February. The travel itinerary may take me to 25 or 30 different cities in a four-week span. For illustrative purposes, here's a 10-day slice out of my calendar during our 1999 recruiting season:

Jan. 15   Gainesville, FL / Blakeley, GA
Jan. 17   Americus, GA
Jan. 18   Kalamazoo, MI / Baltimore, MD
Jan. 19   El Paso, TX
Jan. 21   Ft. Lauderdale / Miami, FL
Jan. 23   Banquet in Tallahassee
Jan. 25   Orlando, FL
Jan. 26   Function at Tallahassee Civic Center
Jan. 27   Pahokee, FL / Evening meeting with Governor Jeb Bush
Jan. 28   Miami, FL

Unlike other years, 1999 wasn't too rough. During one stretch in my 2001 recruiting schedule, I traveled all day from Florida to California, flew back to Florida that evening, left for Texas the next day, and returned that evening to south Florida for visits in several cities. And all this happened on the day after I returned from coaching the Hula Bowl in Hawaii.

In April and May 1999, when I visited various groups on my annual "Booster Tour," my schedule looked like this:

Apr. 10	After spring football game, fly to Orlando, FL
Apr. 11	Home
Apr. 12	Office in Tallahassee
Apr. 13	St. Petersburg, FL
Apr. 14	Midland, TX
Apr. 15	Office in Tallahassee
Apr. 16	Panama City, FL
Apr. 17	Orlando, FL
Apr. 18	Speak to church in Jacksonville, FL
Apr. 19	Jacksonville, FL
Apr. 20	Lake City, FL
Apr. 21	Office in Tallahassee
Apr. 22	Jacksonville, FL
Apr. 23	Atlanta, GA
Apr. 24	Destin, FL
Apr. 25	Speak to church in Wakulla Springs, FL
Apr. 26	Office in Tallahassee
Apr. 27	Marianna, FL
Apr. 28	Memphis, TN
Apr. 29	Office in Tallahassee
Apr. 30	Ft. Lauderdale, FL
May 1	Palm Beach, FL
May 2	Speak to church in Monk's Corner, SC
May 3	Ocala, FL
May 4	Gainesville, FL
May 5	Office in Tallahassee
May 6	Bradenton, FL
May 7	Miami and Ft. Myers, FL
May 8	Home / Office
May 9	Home
May 10	Orange Park, FL
May 11-12	New York

By the end of May each year, my hectic travel schedule ends. Except for speaking engagements, I spend June playing golf with friends, coaching a one-week football camp with my sons, and going on the family vacation. My wife and I might take two weeks to travel somewhere together in mid-July, but otherwise I'm back in the office for various appointments and meetings. Our annual week-long staff meeting is held the last week of July, then we hit the ground running in August when the fall football season begins.

That's a sampling of life as a major college football coach.

My sons Tommy and Terry used to phone me frequently. Then they too became major college head coaches and suddenly they quit calling – except for brief calls on their mobile phones before heading off to the next appointment.

Leadership can make heavy demands on your schedule. The danger is that the extra demands may drag you away from what made you successful in the first place.

✳

Let me tell you some of the things I do to manage my time efficiently:

1. I delegate responsibilities to my assistant coaches.

There's no need for me to deal with every little problem that arises among our football players or in the office. If a boy isn't going to class, I want his position coach to deal with it. I certainly want to know about the problem at our next staff meeting, but I don't have time to deal with it. If a player has been reporting late to meetings, the position coach can discipline him within the guidelines we've established among ourselves.

Players can visit me in my office if they wish. And I'll address any issue that my coaches cannot handle themselves. But otherwise, I empower my coaches to handle most player issues themselves. And I announce this decision to my players.

Likewise among the coaches, I'll let the offensive and defensive coordinators deal with certain issues pertaining to the coaches who work beneath them. Any staff member, of course, can come to my office with his concerns.

There are nine of those assistant coaches, and only one of me. It only makes sense that I hand over to them many of the responsibilities I'd normally assume myself.

Delegation isn't as easy as it sounds, however. If I empower my coaches to deal with certain problems and issues on their own, then I must trust their judgment and support their decisions. One of them might handle a player situation differently than I would handle it. But if I start undermining their decisions, pretty soon they'll just start tossing the problems back to me, which is something I don't have time for.

I need those guys to help me manage my time wisely. Several times in this book you'll hear me say that *I coach the coaches, and they coach the players*. If I can do a good job coaching my coaches, I'll have more time for the other items on my schedule.

Any coach who works long enough in our system is fully prepared to go out and become a good head coach. Goodness, he's already doing many of the jobs associated with the position.

2. Staff meetings are the occasion when most issues are presented to me.

I tell my coaches that unless a problem requires my immediate attention, save it until the upcoming staff meeting. At the meeting, we will collectively determine the best course of action for a particular problem, and then someone at the meeting will be responsible for handling the issue.

The frequency of our staff meetings varies during the year. During our busiest times, I hold staff meetings daily. In the off-season, we meet once or twice a week. I don't want any more meetings than I need to get the job done, but we meet as often as necessary.

3. My work is prioritized.

Winning football games is obviously the key to my job security, so coaching is my number-one priority. During the football season, I won't allow too many extracurricular items to crowd my schedule. I need the time to watch film, meet with staff, map strategies, and attend football practice. Aside from university responsibilities and an occasional speaking engagement at churches on Sundays, I guard this time very jealously. Otherwise, I might be out of a job.

Recruiting season is another time when my schedule must be kept clean. NCAA rules allow the head coach only one off-campus visit with each high school prospect. I go wherever my coaches and I feel that my visit is most needed, and some of those visits are not determined until a few days in advance. My schedule must be kept free for these visits.

All this having been said, I still suffer from an overburdened schedule during the fall football season. Many people wonder why

I – or Joe Paterno and others like us – don't wear headsets throughout a game and call all the plays ourselves. Well, I can't speak for
my peers, but I bet they have the same problem I have. I no longer
have as much free time as I once did to watch film and get prepared for games. Back in our early days at Florida State, I had
plenty of time to prepare myself for a game. Heck, we were losers.
Nobody called to ask if I would come and speak to their organization. I watched film tirelessly and held brainstorming sessions
until I knew everything there was to know about an opponent.
Then on game day, I would don the headsets and make all the calls
from the sidelines.

It ain't that way anymore. Too many people want me to be in too
many places before and after practice. I'd rather watch film and get
ready for the next game. The more I'm taken away from the film
room, the less I can be involved in play calling during the game.

These infringements during football season caused me some real
frustration. I feared they would cause me to lose ballgames. I've
learned, however, that such infringements cannot entirely be avoid-
ed, and I'd better learn to deal with them as efficiently as possible.

I solved the problem by turning the play calling over to my offensive coordinator. He now has my old job of watching film endlessly. I'll watch film, too, during every free moment. The coordinator and I will work together on our game plan, right up until
game day. And I retain veto power over any suggestion he has. But
he is undoubtedly in a better position than I to know which plays
will work best on offense. Until or unless my schedule changes, my
offensive coordinator will call plays during our ballgames.

4. My personal goal is to begin each week with a clean desk.

If necessary, I go into the office on Sunday to review mail from the previous week. My desk is usually clean on Monday morning. I try to keep it that way each day.

Sometimes the work really backs up. I personally answer all of the mail I read, and I personally autograph all the pictures, footballs, caps, helmets, posters, and other paraphernalia requiring my signature. I know one former head coach who used injured players to do his autographing. I guess he figured that no one would be the wiser. I won't do that. All my autographs come from my own hand. But it means my office may get cluttered with hundreds of items on any given day.

Some people say they're just too busy to keep a clean desk. Well, wait a few years. At some point you'll get tired of that excuse and do something about the problem. Then your desk will get a whole lot cleaner.

5. I meet with my secretary daily.

She usually has a long list of items that need my attention. I, in turn, inform her of things I need done that day. These meetings not only help me stay on top of things, but they also help me to keep my desk clean.

9
THE ART OF
PERSUASION

When I was at Alabama, the bumper stickers read "Beat Auburn."
When I was at West Virginia, they read "Beat Pitt." When I
came to FSU, the bumper stickers read "Beat Anybody."
Man, I had a real sales job ahead of me.

As a leader, you are the mouthpiece for your organization. Folks are eager to know what you have to say. They assume you know more about your organization than anyone else, since you're the person in charge.

As a result, you, more than anyone else, are expected to articulate your organization's vision and generate support for its activities. Whether you are asked to raise investment capital, sell your company's product, solicit support from your primary stakeholders, entice prospective employees to join the firm, motivate a sales force, or win the hearts of 19-year-old athletes, your powers of persuasion will be called upon.

Salesmanship is a major component of modern college football. I've been selling since I was 23 years old. And, contrary to public perception, a coach's target market is not limited to high school seniors.

As I mentioned, when I arrived at Florida State in January 1976, the football team had compiled a dismal record over the three previous years. The program barely escaped being terminated by the university president after the 1975 season. Alumni enthusiasm was at an all-time low. I think the average attendance at home games had dropped to around 12,000 fans.

The lack of support had me so worried that once, when a fan called to ask what time our first ballgame started, I answered, *Well, when can you get here?*

Our program faced a serious credibility crisis. And the odds for success were heavily against us. When we played at Miami in 1976, their band played the Miami school anthem and three referees held their hands over their hearts!

Okay, okay. Maybe I'm exaggerating a bit. Still, I had to sell, and sell hard.

My players had to believe that if they followed my plan and did things my way, they could be winners. These kids had forgotten how good it feels to win. They'd forgotten what it's like to hear the crowd screaming in delight. If I could not sell my players on my new vision for FSU football, I was in trouble from the start.

FSU boosters and alumni also had to be sold on the idea. We needed their financial support. Our stadium looked like a tinkertoy erector set. The locker rooms, weight room, and coaches' offices were a cinderblock throwback to the 1950s. My goodness, we were expected to recruit kids who'd just returned from visiting the opulent facilities at Florida, Tennessee, and Alabama. Talk about an uphill battle. No way we could compete with our rivals without competitive facilities. That's like selling record players to kids raised on computers. It just won't work. At FSU, we needed immediate financial support. These alumni had to be brought on board in a hurry.

But the sales effort didn't end there. We also needed our fans to attend the home football games. That's a tall order when you don't have many fans to start with. Some folks don't become fans until you start winning. We couldn't wait that long. We needed fans now, not later. Our kids needed to hear lions roaring in the stands. Then maybe the players would dig their own claws into the dirt and refuse to be beaten. Curious onlookers had to be sold on their value to our team's success.

I also had to sell the media. Sportswriters were – and still are – my medium of communication with the general public. Their daily articles on the sports page remain my single most important life-line to FSU fans throughout Florida. Most folks know only what they read in the newspaper. So you can believe I granted interviews whenever asked.

Finally, and of equal importance, I had to sell young high school seniors and their parents on the benefits of attending Florida State University.

I became a full-time salesman for Florida State University. The task couldn't be delegated to someone else. *I* was the spokesperson for Florida State football. Selling the program was my first and most critical job. And I was not in a position to be argumentative with the media, aloof from the general public, at odds with my players, or prone to bouts of bad temperament. Woe unto me if I lost sight of my responsibility as point man on the sales team.

✳

The first T-shirts I recall seeing upon my arrival at Florida State in 1976 proclaimed *It All Begins with Bowden.*

Talk about pressure!

✳

Don't use smoke and mirrors when you visit a prospect. If you believe in what you're doing, and if you have something good to offer someone, then there should be no need to stretch the truth or embellish the facts. Go with what you've got. Highlight what you do best. And always focus on how your organization will benefit the person being sold.

When my coaches and I first recruited players to Florida State in 1976, we sold parents and athletes on our friendliness and accessibility. That may sound weak, but we didn't have much else to offer. We had no tradition. Few people knew about us. Our facilities were inadequate and outdated. But there were some things we could surely do, and we could do them better than anyone else. We could look after these players while they were with us. We could listen to their problems and show them that we care. So what if other schools did the same thing? We would do it better. Every momma and daddy could rest content that their child was in our hands. And I meant every word of my new sales message.

Believe me, I INSISTED that my staff be caring and accessible. If a player came to see me about a problem, I would interrupt my meeting to talk with him. If a boy got homesick, I put my arm around him and talked to him as though I were talking to my own son. My assistant coaches were expected to do the same. If attentiveness and concern for players is what we sold them on, then dadgum it, we'd better be as good as our word.

✳

Don't do something to make a sale if you know it's illegal. And don't do it if your conscience or common sense tells you otherwise. I understand the temptation to cheat. Just trust me on this one.

We've all heard stories of coaches who cut corners or offered improper incentives. It seems that someone each year adds his name to the list of convicted cheaters. And once that stain gets on your hands, it's awfully difficult to wash off.

I've certainly had opportunities to make a sale by dishonest means. One Sunday afternoon I visited the home of a player in northeast Florida. The boy's father was a minister, which pleased me immensely. I talked with him at length about Christian faith and the role that religion plays in my coaching philosophy. I enjoy such conversations because I once considered entering the ministry. Even now, I take my players to church twice a year – once to a predominantly black church, and once to a predominantly white church – all the while encouraging them to participate in some campus religious organization on a regular basis.

Naturally, I hoped the minister would want his son to attend Florida State. But what he did next caught me off guard. In a very roundabout way, the father asked about his son's chances of getting a new car. I stiffened. As I continued to listen, it became obvious that some coach from another school had offered the boy a vehicle if he would sign with them. The father was feeling me out on the same subject.

The conversation became awkward for both of us. When he finished talking, I politely told him what I've told others: *Here's what we can offer your son. Anything more is improper and cannot be done. If someone has told you otherwise, they are wrong.* Our visit drew to a close, and I returned to Tallahassee with a feeling of indifference toward this player. One month later, the boy signed a scholarship with another school. I didn't care.

We coaches can tell when someone else has tried to induce a player with improper gifts, because the player or his family will feel us out to see if we can equal or better the offer. I tell my coaches to steer clear of these conversations: *Tell them what we are allowed to offer and offer nothing more. If the family persists, then walk away and forget the kid.*

✳

My advice to leaders is to write a good three- to five-point summary of your sales message that you can recite forwards and backwards in two minutes. A 10-point summary is too long. Nobody can remember 10 points. But they will remember three, and maybe five.

That summary is your base message. Everything else you say should work off that base.

In football, we have what are called base formations. During a game, the quarterback may take a snap under center and then turn around to face his two running backs in the I-formation. From that point forward, and out of that I-formation alignment, the quarterback can do a number of different things. He can hand off to the fullback on a dive play. He can option to the tailback. He can fake the dive play and drop back to pass. Or he can run a flanker reverse. A number of plays work off that base I-formation alignment. The play selected will depend on how the defense has lined up against us.

Likewise, once you have your base message, you can ad-lib as needed in a particular circumstance.

✳

I listen carefully to what the players and parents reveal to me. Selling most often comes down to listening to their concerns or identifying their priorities.

I also tell the parents I'll watch over their son while he is in my program. Parents have a natural anxiety about their child's departure from home. A lot of bad things can happen to a young person when he's first out on his own. I convey my sincere aim to watch over that young man, provide him with a good environment in which to get his education, and protect him from certain dangers he may confront.

Perhaps if I was only selling a wrench to a plumber in a hardware store, this personal dimension wouldn't be important. But some sales jobs require that people believe in you and trust that you will do in the future what you say you'll do today.

Nothing wins trust like a good track record. If I can demonstrate to parents that I'm a man who keeps his word, my words carry more weight. So I guess I'd say to a young leader that you should begin establishing a track record of keeping your word and taking care of your troops. If folks in your organization can say, *Yes, he made the same promise to me 10 years ago, and he was true to his word*, more has been said than can ever be portrayed on a spreadsheet or a sales pamphlet.

That's another reason not to blow smoke and make embellished promises that you know you cannot keep. If you fudge the truth, you set yourself up for the charge of not keeping your promises. You may get short-term results, but deception and dishonesty will hurt your reputation in the long run.

✳

Be realistic when you go out to sell. Know your limits.

When I was at Samford University in the early 1960s, I didn't need to compete against Alabama and Auburn for recruits. Samford was a small, independent NAIA school. We didn't play in the SEC, and we didn't need SEC-caliber players. We only needed players good enough to beat our NAIA opponents.

Did I want to sign some Parade All-Americans for Samford University? Sure I did. Would it have made me feel like a million bucks to steal one or two of them out from under Alabama's nose? Sure it would. But why waste my time and the school's money going after them? Alabama would get them if it wanted them.

I spent my time recruiting in my target market. We could win with Alabama's leftovers, and we had a good chance of luring those leftovers to Samford.

Heck, I would go to the University of Alabama each spring and sit in on staff meetings. Their coaches, including Bear Bryant, were very helpful. I learned a lot of football from them. And on more than one occasion, they steered a player my way.

✳

Is it possible to do too good a job winning a customer's heart?

Back in the early 1970s, while I was the head coach at WVU, I visited a player down in southern West Virginia who was from a very poor background. The kid was All-Everything in high school, and I wanted him badly. My goodness, he was a home-grown star, and I coached the only major university in his state. This boy needed to attend West Virginia University.

The young man's family didn't have many worldly goods, and they lived out in the middle of nowhere. To get to his house, I had to get off the paved road and drive about a mile up a winding one-lane dirt road into a hollow between the mountains. There was no other way in . . . no other way out . . . and no other houses along the way.

The dusty drive ended in front of a small frame house. I went in, met the family, and spent some quality time with the boy's father. He was clearly the decision-maker in the family. One of my assistant coaches had already visited on several occasions. He thought the father might be a moonshiner who sold white whiskey back in these mountains. The man looked pretty rugged to me. He didn't mince words, but he did shoot straight. And what with me being an old southern boy, we hit it off very well. He clearly seemed to like me.

Now, at that time, Jerry Claiborne was the head coach at the University of Maryland. Jerry and I had been good friends since the days when I was at Samford and he was an assistant for Bear Bryant at Alabama. I knew Jerry was coming here the next day on a recruiting visit. So as I was leaving the house, I turned to the father and said half-jokingly, *Now listen. Coach Claiborne from Maryland will be coming by here tomorrow on a recruiting visit. Don't let that rascal come in here and steal your son out from under our noses.*

As I turned to walk away, the father deadpanned, *Well, if he does, I'll kill him!*

I laughed, waved goodbye, and kept walking, wondering all the while if I should call Jerry.

Driving home, I felt my chances of getting this kid were pretty good.

❋

Be sincere. Sell your strengths. Don't promise something you can't give – or don't have a right to offer.

And stay away from that kid in West Virginia, or I'll tell his dad.

10

HIRING

←—————————————————→

My first requirement of a new employee is Loyalty, Loyalty, Loyalty.

Loyalty is my number-one criterion for each prospective employee.

Coaching is a tough business. If we can't stick together, we've got big problems. I make this very clear when I hire someone.

When I took the head coaching job at Florida State in 1976, my coaches and I held the most significant staff meeting of my career at FSU. We met to decide what kind of program we would create. After tedious and intense hours in meetings, we hammered out our strategy.

At the top of our list was the resolution that coaches must put the team first. Any player or staff member who would not comply with this objective was dead weight and would have to go.

I am convinced that a staff cannot build the proper chemistry within its organization unless the staff is committed to the team concept. The *team* – both coaches and players together – is more important than any individual. This team mentality, or team chemistry, is at the heart of our success at Florida State. And it begins with the assistant coaches. They are the ones who instill the team concept in our players.

Consequently, success begins with hiring coaches who put the welfare of FSU and its players ahead of everything else. My coaches are asked to assume a deep responsibility to our players that goes far beyond football. We want these boys to find help academically and spiritually, as well as learn how to play winning football. As a team, we must study together, play together, and pray together. This approach builds for success long after football is over.

If I don't believe a prospective coach can be loyal to my team philosophy, I will not hire him.

✻

Coaching isn't that difficult. I can teach a guy how to coach. So when I'm interviewing a prospective staff member, I ask myself about the things I cannot teach him:

Can he relate to our players?

Can he get along with the rest of the staff?

Is he a good, moral man who won't do anything to get our program in trouble?

My job as the head coach is to coach the coaches. I'll make sure a new coach is doing things the way I want them done. In turn, my coaches will coach the players. But these coaches must *fit* within my system.

✻

In my profession, the head coach makes the hiring decision on each member of the coaching staff. If you have a large company with hundreds of employees, you or your CEO may not know who has been hired into certain positions. Sometimes it's just not practical for the chief officers to review resumes, conduct interviews, and negotiate terms. Even so, I advise you as a leader to stay informed about prospective new employees. They determine the productivity of your business. Poor performance may lead to retaliation by the company's stakeholders. And in most cases, the axe falls first on management's neck. In the business of college football, substitute *head(less) coach* for *management*.

✻

Bear Bryant taught me back in the early 1960s that if I wanted to build a winning program, I must first surround myself with winners. He advised me to hire men who were eager, energetic, hardworking, and hungry for the same thing I wanted.

I've modified the Bear's sage advice over the past 40 years. Here's what I look for in any prospective new coach:

- ✗ Loyalty
- ✗ Good character
- ✗ Ambition
- ✗ Dependability
- ✗ Hardworking
- ✗ Good attitude
- ✗ Goal-oriented

Notice I didn't mention *experience*. It's not that experience is unimportant. I won't hire someone into a full-time position who has never coached a down of football. That would be foolish. I need someone who can step right in and get going from day one, and this requires a considerable familiarity with coaching.

But I like home-grown coaches. I'll take a young guy with little or no coaching experience – maybe a former player or a young high school coach – and slowly bring him up within our system. Perhaps he'll learn the ropes as a volunteer assistant, graduate assistant, or recruiting coordinator. Then, when I have an opening, I'll promote him into a full-time position.

I'm not particularly interested in filling vacancies with the most experienced, successful coach in the business. I know what I want done in my program. What I need are people capable of carrying out the plan.

The one exception has been my coordinators. I need guys from established winning programs to coordinate my offense and defense – guys who have been there before and know the sweet taste of success. I'll fill either of these jobs with a guy from my own staff, if possible. Otherwise, I'll go outside our program to find the right person. But he must be someone who comes from a winning program.

❋

If you don't hire a person with good character, then you'd better hope he's dumb and lazy. If he's smart and energetic, he will get you in all kinds of trouble.

✳

I prefer to hire ambitious men who want to be head coaches. Guys like that have their own ideas and aren't afraid to express them. They'll challenge me if they think I'm wrong, or if they know a better way to get things done. And as long as they disagree in the right spirit, I prefer it that way. They'll also allow me to challenge their thinking without cowering under the boss's glare.

Here's what I mean by hiring ambitious, confident staff members. During a game, if we're backed up to our own 5-yard line on second-and-ten, and my offensive coordinator wants to call a pass play to the split end out in the flat, I'm worried. Second-and-ten is an obvious passing down. How about a draw play, or a swing pass to the halfback? If the defense intercepts the ball out there in the flat, it's an easy touchdown.

So I'll grab a headphone and ask him, *Are you sure it will work? You've studied the film more than I have. You work with our quarterbacks during practice. Can the quarterback make the throw? Do we have the right receiver in the game for that play? How deep are their cornerbacks playing off the line of scrimmage? Don't call that dadgum play if you think we might get it intercepted.*

Now a timid offensive coordinator might get scared and back off of his original suggestion. My questions in the heat of battle may have him more worried about my wrath than about the best call. I just want him to make the best call under the circumstances. He's watched more film on our opponent than I have. I expect him to have good answers to my questions. If my challenge intimidates him – makes him back off *out of fear* and call a very conservative play that nets only one yard – then I need another guy up there in the pressbox calling plays.

I need someone with conviction who is not afraid of being challenged. I win with men of conviction.

✳

Don't hire someone just because he's your buddy. Always ask yourself, *Can he do what I need him to do? Can he get along with the other coaches? Will he work hard? Will he accept his role?* One of the biggest employment mistakes I ever made was hiring a guy because I felt sorry for him. He'd been through a lot of personal hardship that was not his fault. He was a hard worker and a happy-go-lucky kind of guy. You couldn't help but like him. But his personal morality turned out to be a real problem, and I ended up having to fire him several years later.

✳

Take your time and do your homework when hiring new employees.

Don't rush your decision. The person you hire will be there a long time, if you hire correctly. Hire the wrong guy in the name of speed, and you'll spend the next two years trying to figure out how to fire him.

You better know what you're getting before you hire him. He may break you.

If I don't already know a prospective coach, I'll call his former head coach. Or I'll call someone else that I trust and ask that person about him. Bad decisions cost me time, energy, and ballgames. I'd rather spend a little extra time on the front end and get a good return on my investment.

Poor hires demonstrate poor judgment on my part.

＊

Whenever I consider hiring someone, I ask myself how the rest of the staff will feel about him. I know what my guys are like. I also know they aren't going to change just because I bring in someone new who has different opinions on certain cherished topics. So I must make a judgment about how well the applicant will fit into the personality of my staff. If he is a defensive line coach, I must determine if he can work well with our defensive coordinator and with the other defensive coaches.

No one benefits if I try to fit a round peg into a square hole. And I don't have time to create new problems for myself.

＊

Look for reasons not to hire the person you're interested in.

If you can't find any good reasons to pass on him, then hire him.

＊

Do not hire "Yes Men." These people will *let* you get in trouble.

＊

You win with the right people properly led.

11

FIRING

←—————————————————————————→

*If I must fire someone, I view the dismissal
as a failure on my part.*

I've only dismissed three coaches during my entire career. I view their dismissals as personal failures on my part, since I made the decisions to hire them. I want my staff members to succeed, so I try not to fire anyone.

Oddly enough, back in the 1980s I had a coach who dared me to fire him.

This particular coach was a passionate man who happened to disagree with something I wanted done during practice. Now, he was a good coach. He pushed the players harder than I would, and he was a bit difficult to get along with on occasion, but he was a great teacher who got a lot out of the kids. His value to my staff was greater than any problems I might have with his occasional outbursts. And he had a lovely wife and beautiful children.

One morning, in the privacy of my office, he argued his point with such passionate indignation that I had to remind him which of us was the head coach. I tried responding to his argument, feeling that his thoughts deserved a fair hearing and a point-by-point response. But in the end, I was unconvinced and maintained my position. This only made him angrier. He dared me to fire him.

If you don't like what I think, then just fire me, he bellowed.

I don't want to fire you, I responded.

I tried to end the conversation as quickly as I knew how, without either of us getting our feathers ruffled any more than they had been. I'm not offended when a person expresses his true convictions, even if his conviction is that I'm dead wrong about something. At the same time, I don't like for someone to issue an ultimatum. Ultimatums take a disagreement to a higher level. Even so, he hadn't done anything to merit dismissal. Whatever other response I might make, firing him would only be a knee-jerk reaction unmerited by the circumstances.

But he was persistent. He argued further, and I once again reminded him that I was the head coach and would do whatever I believed was best for our team. My response merely stoked the coals of his discontent. Again he dared me to fire him.

Finally, in total exasperation, I told him, *Coach, I don't want to fire you. But if you insist on being fired, then put your resignation in writing, come back in here and give it to me, and I'll accept it. Otherwise, I'm the head coach and we're doing it my way. You understand, however, that your resignation is not what I want. I want you to stay and keep doing the job you've been doing. But if you feel you can't work here anymore, then I'll accept your resignation.*

Well, by this point he was in tears. Obviously he had been under a lot of stress. Firing him for insubordination would've been the wrong thing to do. He left the office and we never had another problem with that particular issue.

＊

I'd be better off telling you what I do to *keep from firing* staff members than how I go about *firing someone.* Those points, however, are found throughout these chapters, particularly in the chapter on "Hiring."

The most important reason for so few dismissals is the fact that I have been fortunate to hire good people. My staff members all profess a strong faith in God, for which I'm thankful. They also are men who have demonstrated good character in their previous jobs. Hiring people of strong moral character doesn't guarantee anything. A person might still turn out differently than I hoped. But it sure gives me good odds.

I also lay down my non-negotiables with each new staff member, and I repeat these non-negotiables every year at our annual hideaway staff meeting. None of us are confused about the minimal conditions for job security. At the very least, these annual repetitions may help one or two folks resist a temptation that might otherwise cost them their jobs. The repetitions also help to clear my conscience. If I repeatedly make it clear that certain behaviors will not be tolerated, and someone then decides to violate a prohibition anyway, the decision to dismiss him cannot be construed as arbitrary.

＊

I'll dismiss a coach for one of four reasons:

1. Illegal conduct.

If a coach cheats to get a player, he knows I will dismiss him from my staff. This issue is discussed every year, and every year I remind them: *If you cheat, I will not support you. Whatever the consequences for you, I will not intervene on your behalf.*

2. Immoral conduct.

I expect good moral living from everyone on my staff. I don't hope for it. I don't wish for it. I expect it. Coaches must set an example for the players. We don't need leaders who live without a moral compass. Immorality cannot and will not be tolerated.

My insistence upon good conduct has not been without regrets. I once fired a coach for getting a divorce from his wife. He was the first coach ever to divorce while on my staff.

At that time in my career, I had never hired a divorced person because I wanted committed family men on my staff. There had been rumors of promiscuous activity by this coach, but those rumors had never been confirmed. I fired him over the divorce.

Looking back, I wish I hadn't done it. Divorce was a serious matter in those days, as far as social acceptance is concerned. And I'm very serious about surrounding myself with men of good moral character. I just look at divorce a little differently today than I once did. I now see it as a personal matter, and I stay out of it.

I did fire one coach for immoral sexual behavior. He was probably lonely or something, I don't know. But I received some complaints, including one from a female member of the university administrative staff. Once that rumor was confirmed, I called him into my office and told him what I knew. I also told him that he could not remain on my staff.

Sexual promiscuity, alcohol abuse, disloyalty, and dishonesty will get a person dismissed. All four are moral issues.

3. Laziness

I cannot win with players who are undependable. Guys who won't come to practice, who skip classes, or who look for excuses to avoid hard work are dead weight.

The same holds true for members of my coaching staff. For our program to run efficiently, everyone must do his job. If I cannot depend on a coach to do what he says he will do, then I'm in trouble. My program is in trouble. My other coaches will resent him if he's lazy. And they'll resent me if I do nothing about it.

4. Can't get along with others.

If a guy just can't get along with the players or with his fellow coaches no matter how hard he tries (or doesn't try, as the case may be), then it's a mistake to keep him on board for very long.

It isn't difficult to tell when there's a serious problem of this nature. If players keep coming into my office, semester after semester, describing a repetitive litany of problems, an accurate pattern will soon emerge. And, of course, I'm with the coaches frequently in staff meetings and at football practice. I can usually see what's going on.

Normally, my first recourse is to discuss these problems privately with the coach. I'll tell him what I've heard – or observed – and we will look for helpful solutions. If an effective solution can't be found, my choices become more limited.

Sometimes, however, a case will arise wherein complaints are made but firing is not the appropriate solution.

I had a situation several years ago in which a coach of mine apparently wasn't getting along very well with his colleagues. The problem arose shortly after I promoted him to a leadership position over the rest of the staff. He was a sharp thinker with a lot of good ideas. And he was one heck of a good organizer. I wanted him as my back-up. But once he was promoted, the complaining began. A number of my coaches resented his demeanor and style. They complained to me individually and privately that he was too "bossy" in his new position. When they weren't openly complaining to me, they expressed themselves by innuendo and insinuation. The situation became very tiresome. I liked this coach, I was tired of hearing the complaints against him, and I was determined to get to the heart of the problem. So I called the entire staff into my office and asked them to lock the door behind them. Then I asked them to sit down, and I said: *Men, a number of you have complained about Coach ____. Well, there he is sitting right in front of you. I want you to speak up and tell him to his face what is wrong with his leadership. You've all been telling ME. Now tell HIM!* Well, every coach – including the man I had promoted – aired their feelings and got everything off their chest. When we finished, some men had tears in their eyes. There were handshakes and hugs. And I never heard another complaint about this coach's leadership methods – in part because he learned some things in that meeting that made him a better leader.

✳

There's no easy way to fire someone, so don't look for one.

A good leader will not take the easy way out, no matter how badly he wants to. The person to be fired may have a wife and children who wonder why dad can't work at his job anymore. His economic livelihood is at stake. The news media may get involved. These facts shouldn't be taken lightly. Some measure of consideration must be maintained.

But when the person must be dismissed, the leader should be resolute. Be sure to have your facts correct. Think through the reasons why the dismissal must occur. Be your own devil's advocate. Have you repeatedly made it clear that the offensive behavior will not be tolerated? Are you guilty of the same offense yourself? If you cannot find sufficient reason to retain the person, then be brief and direct. Cite your reasons. People can deal with the truth. They don't deal as well with mamby-pamby ambiguity.

If I absolutely must fire a coach, I will call him in my office and say, in effect, *Coach, you've done such-and-such, which you know I will not tolerate. I'm gonna have to let you go.*

I hate to fire anyone. It hurts me because I care for my coaches and their wives and children. But once it's done, I feel the weight lifted from my shoulders.

✳

Firing should be done when it's the best solution for everyone involved.

It sounds strange to suggest that firing could be in the best interest of the person being let go. But it's true. Sometimes the most unfair thing you can do to a person is to allow him to continue his employment after the situation has become untenable.

I once had an assistant coach whom I had inherited from an earlier staff. After working with him a year, I noticed he couldn't discipline players. He was a poor teacher. He never prepared extensively. And I could tell his players didn't respect him.

I called him into my office and told him he needed to be in another profession because he was not a coach. He resigned and went on to become a very prosperous businessman. I'm happy for him. And I know he's pleased with what's become of his life after football.

When you fire someone, you don't have the benefit of knowing how the future will turn out for him. But sometimes people just choose the wrong profession, or the wrong position, and it's simply unfair to let it continue. Their skills are better suited for something else.

✳

Demotions sometimes work as well as firing.

I once had a coach who just didn't possess the right chemistry to deal with our athletes. Players kept coming into my office complaining about their relationship with him. The problem was clear to me as well. It was serious enough to demand my response, but, as I've said, I hate firing someone if I don't have to.

My solution was to call him into my office and say, "*Coach, I'm reassigning you because . . .*" (and I cited the reasons). I knew he wouldn't like the demotion, and he didn't. Two weeks later he resigned to take another job.

Instead of our relationship turning nasty, it ended amicably. I pushed him, but he chose to make the leap. We both could claim some measure of satisfaction with our decisions.

✳

Not all firings occur for the right reasons. Sometimes it's really the boss who needs to be fired. Perhaps the boss is threatened by a highly effective subordinate. Or the boss needs a scapegoat to atone for his own mismanagement. Or the boss makes demands that no reasonable person will satisfy. Such individuals may be bosses, but they are lousy leaders.

I've seen head coaches fire staff members when they should've fired themselves. Firing a staff member might make the head coach look decisive in the eyes of the athletic director, president, and key boosters. But more often than not, I think firing an assistant makes the head coach look bad. After all, the head coach is the person who hired him. Is his judgment really that bad?

12
STAFF MEETINGS

←————————————————→

If everyone agrees with me on every issue,
then someone isn't needed.

Staff meetings are the single most important component of my management strategy. They allow me to stay on top of things within my organization.

The frequency of our staff meetings varies through the year. We meet every morning during spring practice (March-April) and during the regular fall season (August-November), reviewing whatever needs to be done that day. During recruiting season (December-February), we meet every Monday and sometimes on Friday. On Mondays we share information gleaned from our visits with recruits on the prior weekend. On Fridays we review the schedules of recruiting visits for the coming weekend.

During the months of May, June, and July, I call meetings only as needed.

Staff meetings convene at 8:30 A.M. Some coaches may want to have breakfast with their families and then take their children to school. I allow them time for morning family responsibilities before the meeting begins.

A staff meeting may last one or two hours, depending on the agenda.

Everyone who has a direct bearing on the success of our program is asked to attend these meetings – our 10 full-time coaches, our graduate and volunteer assistant coaches, the trainers, equipment managers, our academic liaison personnel, and anyone else from whom I might need information. We might have as many as 17 people in the meeting. Some of these people, such as the trainers or academic liaison personnel, will be dismissed after giving their reports to the coaches.

When the meeting is over, we all have sufficient information to get our daily jobs done, and I know what's going on in my organization.

＊

We begin every staff meeting with a devotional and prayer. My coaches and trainers are asked to take turns leading the devotional. We print out a devotional schedule and post it on the wall in our meeting room so that everyone knows when it's his turn.

Devotionals are limited to two or three minutes. Members are asked to use personal anecdotes, biblical passages, or perhaps something they read in a book or magazine as the focus of the devotional. Then the staff member closes with a prayer. If he is not comfortable with this request, then I will lead the prayer myself.

Devotionals set a healthy boundary around our staff meetings and our work relationships. Football is a very competitive sport.

Tempers can flare. Office jealousies can arise. Problems can beset us from the outside. And there are the myriad personal problems we all bring with us to work.

Devotionals have a healing and comforting effect. It's difficult to stay mad at a colleague when you hear him talking about his love for his sick father, or when he explains how a passage of scripture has helped him through a difficult time. The devotional time reminds us that life is much bigger than football, no matter how passionately we feel about our jobs or how hard we work to win.

Devotionals give us PERSPECTIVE. Once the devotional ends, we go to the first item of business on our agenda.

I cannot emphasize strongly enough how valuable these devotionals are to the tone and temper of our organization. But I can tell you a story of how one outsider evaluated them.

It's a Florida State – Nebraska story, starring Nebraska's former head football coach and current U.S. congressman, Tom Osborne. It should be noted at the beginning that Tom has always been a devout Christian. Through the course of our two careers, Christian faith has meant as much to him as it has to me. Tom has always taken his faith to work. He's a man who practices what he preaches.

Back in the late 1980s and early 1990s, our FSU teams had beaten Nebraska five straight times in regular season and bowl games. The last of those wins was for the national championship in 1993, which we won 18-16 in the Orange Bowl. Nebraska had great teams during that span. But for some reason, we just happened to have their number. Tom Osborne was taking a lot of heat in the media about never being able to win a national championship. The criticism seems ridiculous when you look back at his record during that time, but he caught flak nonetheless.

I knew what he was going through. The same things were said about me right up until '93, when I finally got the monkey off my back with the help of Charlie Ward.

After that '93 championship game, Tom called me and asked if he could visit with our coaches in Tallahassee during our 1994 spring practice. He wanted to know what we were doing that he wasn't.

He came and stayed a week in March 1994. He attended all our staff meetings, visited with our assistant coaches, and attended our practices and team meetings. Then he returned to Nebraska and won three of the next four national championships, including back-to-back titles in '94 and '95.

Now here's the point of the story. Tom later commented that the only difference he could find between our two programs was the devotional we held at the beginning of our staff meetings. So in 1994, he installed devotionals at the beginning of his own staff meetings. Isn't it interesting that the two most successful programs of the past two decades give such high priority to religious faith? Tom said it best when he wrote:

The common perception of football coaches is that of hard-driving, profane, callous individuals who care little about spiritual matters. Often people engaged in highly competitive enterprises believe that matters of faith hinder effective performance. My experience has led me to believe that spiritual preparation contributes to effective performance no matter what the arena.[i]

---

[i] Tom Osborne, *Faith in the Game*. Broadway Books: New York, 1999.

Religion isn't magic. Devotionals don't mean that God favors us more than he favors our opponents. God won't cause us to win just because we pray. But genuine faith has an enormous impact on the way we work together and the way we work with our players. Faith makes us better coaches because it helps us to keep our jobs in perspective. We learn not to worry about things over which we have no control. And we remain focused on the things that matter most.

I have no idea how many problems we've managed to avoid because of the love, courage, determination, and mutual support that our devotionals have generated among staff and players.

*

The foundation of your leadership persona is laid in staff meetings.

Why?

Because, odds are, the staff receives your full attention more frequently in staff meetings than at any other time. Here is where they witness first-hand how you deal with issues and solve problems. Here is where they hear your personal thoughts. Nowhere is your true demeanor more evident.

They are more apt to see the REAL you during these regular staff meetings than in any other venue. And they are drawing conclusions about you at every meeting. If you're phony, they'll spot it quickly. If you're unorganized, or lack communication skills, or are disingenuous or hypocritical, here's where they learn about it.

You win or lose the leadership game in these meetings, because if you can't lead these folks, you'll never lead the folks beneath them.

We normally think of staff meetings as management functions rather than leadership functions. But good management is a vital aspect of leadership. Name a well-known leader who is not also a manager and I'll eat my words. I can't think of any.

Good leaders *manage* to succeed. They *manage* to keep everyone headed in the right direction. They *manage* to establish good morale.

If nothing else, good leaders are good managers.

*

Here are some of my operative management principles for staff meetings:

1. Never meet longer or more frequently than you must – but when you meet, get everything done that needs to be done. This is the most frequently violated principle of staff meetings.

2. Prepare a list of objectives before entering the meeting.

I hate having to attend a meeting when the person who called it isn't prepared. He just wings it until someone says something interesting, and then he wants to talk about it for the next 45 minutes. I don't have time for that kind of stuff, and neither does my staff.

3. Be in charge of the meeting. I tell my staff members that we each have voting privileges on any matter before us. All nine of them have one vote each. I have 10 votes.

I do, however, encourage independence of thought among my staff members. If everybody agrees with me on every issue, then someone isn't needed.

I want my coaches to express their convictions. I don't mind someone challenging me on an issue, provided we're courteous and tact-
ful with one another. I call this "disagreeing agreeably." Staff meetings, however, are not permitted to become argumentative free-
for-alls. My job is to keep the meeting headed in a productive
direction. Plus, I have those 10 votes!

4. Do your coaching in the staff meeting.

As I've said before, I coach the coaches and my coaches coach the
players.

5. Never berate or belittle a staff member in front of his peers. It
absolutely kills morale and creates a bad environment in which to work.

If you've got to express disapproval over a staff member's actions,
find a way to do it that is caring rather than despotic.

I prefer a baton to a big stick.

I might ask a staff member, *What was the problem on the field yesterday? I thought we agreed to do such-and-such, and it didn't look
like we were doing it.* Or if two very competitive coaches exchanged
words in front of our players the previous day, I might say to the
entire staff, *Men, we've got a responsibility to set an example for our
players. If we bicker on the practice field, we're not being very good role
models. So let's be real careful to watch that next time.*

My comments are normally addressed to the entire staff. A guy
will usually know if I'm talking more directly about him.

My staff knows, because I tell them on numerous occasions, that
if a couple of them don't get along with each other, then I will

decide which one must leave. I'm not going to put up with internal turmoil.

6. Do not be late to scheduled meetings, especially if you called the meeting.

If I had a habit of arriving late or at unpredictable times, it would send a message that starting times aren't all that important to me. It would also appear that I cannot manage my time very well. Either way, I would be wasting my staff's time as they sat around waiting for me to show up.

7. Don't call others to a meeting if you can handle matters alone in a more efficient manner.

13
EVALUATING PERFORMANCE

The greatest mistake is to continue practicing a mistake.

Several years ago, I was driving along a familiar Alabama highway when I noticed my gas gauge hovering near empty. Immediately I began watching the roadside billboards for information about the nearest gas station.

One particular billboard caught my eye. It was an advertisement for a gas and convenience store under new management. The proud owners issued the following invitation to motorists:

Stop in and try our hamburgers. Eat a chili dog. Get gas.

Well, I had a long drive ahead of me, and I definitely needed a fill-up. But I was a little concerned that if I stopped in I might drive out of there with more gas than I intended to purchase.

After 71 years, I still marvel at how often our best effort to communicate can become a paradigm of miscommunication. On almost any given occasion, two people can have a conversation and walk away with two very different interpretations of what was just resolved.

Confusion over what we mean to say is partly due to ambiguities in our language. How can *a slim chance* and *a fat chance* be the same, while *a wise man* and *a wise guy* are opposites? And how can *overlook* and *oversee* be opposites, while *quite a lot* and *quite a few* are alike?

Confusion arises most frequently, however, when we don't take sufficient measures to be clear about what we mean to say, or else we don't repeat it often enough.

When it comes to evaluating the performance of my individual staff members, I've learned two very important lessons over the years.

First, I must clearly articulate my expectations, and then repeat those expectations on a regular basis.

Several times in this book I have referenced our annual hideaway meeting in July. My hideaway notes have expanded over the years into the size of a working manual. It's easily over 100 pages at this point.

Each coach receives a copy of our hideaway notes at the beginning of the meeting. We then go through the document page by page.

One section deals with our goals for the year. Another identifies the responsibilities each coach will have during the season – one coach is our liaison with game officials, another oversees the player's training table, and another is responsible for knowing the rules applicable to exchanging game film with other ACC schools. On and on we go, through every phase of the upcoming year, with each coach receiving specific responsibilities related to the operation of our program. Those assignments constitute concrete criteria by which their performance is evaluated.

The hideaway notes also outline more general expectations that apply the same to all coaches. These expectations reflect my general philosophy of coaching. Because these expectations are also criteria by which I evaluate performance, they must be made clear. Here are just a few points I make each year during hideaway:

✗ You win with the right people properly led.

✗ You get better, or you get worse. You never remain the same. Sell the players on this.

✗ Don't depend on the undependables.

✗ Once you take it for granted that you are going to have a great team because you have great talent, you've got problems. You must coach that talent.

✗ Every decision I make is predicated upon the question *How does it affect team morale?*

✗ Our staff must support and care for one another. The offensive and defensive coordinators must play a big role. The key to squad morale is staff morale.

✗ You as a coach must be sure we do not lose because the opponent is more fundamentally sound than us (blocking and tackling technique), or because we have a poor scheme that allows mistakes.

✘ Coordinators have the final say-so. If you feel the coordinator's decision is wrong or unfair, then you and the coordinator come see me.

✘ Know what academic courses, and how many credit hours, your players are taking each semester. Don't depend on, or blame, someone else if you don't have the information. Get your players to give you their schedules.

✘ If we don't get second effort from our players, it's because coaches are not demanding it. Second effort is coachable and can be disciplined.

✘ You may fuss and argue about what we're going to do, but once we settle on a plan, we all pull together.

✘ We must be loyal to one another, to the athletic director, to the president of the university, and to FSU.

My hideaway notes include many pages of these general expectations. We cover them one by one. And we cover them each year. I believe that people cannot be held accountable unless they know what is expected of them. My job is to ensure that those expectations are clearly enumerated.

Second, if I assign tasks to others, their style will be different from mine. I must allow for these differences. A coach can be just as effective as me – or even more effective – doing things his way. It would be foolish to evaluate his performance in comparison with the way I might handle a situation.

My longtime defensive coordinator is a case in point. He was an All-American defensive back under Bear Bryant at Alabama back in the early 1960s. Like me, he was raised on tough-nosed football. He also has been a head coach before, so he understands about leadership.

Our two personalities are very different. So are our styles. He is intense during practice, and his emotive demeanor carries over onto the sidelines during a game. He's a perfectionist who demands the absolute best from his players. And around Tallahassee, he is well known for the litany of biting one-liners he'll use during practice to correct an errant player. Here's a sampling of his comments:

Son, I've got to call your momma and apologize. I told her you were a good football player.

Son, you've got a good engine, but your hands aren't on the steering wheel.

Get off my field. You're stinking up the place.

Players sometimes laugh when recalling their humbling experiences with him, because they've learned that he cares for them. The freshmen aren't sure at first. His vitriolic assessment of their performance leaves little doubt that they have a long way to go. But once they're around a while, they recognize his method for what it is. He makes them better players.

Sometimes I have to be the good guy to his bad guy. I'll occasionally step in and say to a player, *Now you know he only gets on a player if he likes him. You keep working hard, because he has his eyes on you.* I would never tell this coach he should do things just the way I would do them. He's got his own style, and it works for him.

As long as my coaches work within the framework of my system, which does include a strong emphasis on our moral obligations to the players and to one another, I will allow for latitude in methods.

✳

I am a hands-on manager.

A tower and a notecard are my two best methods of evaluating performance.

I attend every practice with a notecard and pen in my back pocket. And I sit up in a tall tower so I can watch everything that's going on. As I watch practice, I take notes. I also take notes during games. That way, I don't forget. If I notice a defensive back out of position, I write it down. My coaches will need to correct that problem. Maybe I notice a lineman has missed a blocking assignment, or the quarterback is throwing off his back foot, or a receiver runs the wrong route, and I write that down, too. Or I notice a coach reacting too harshly or failing to teach something we discussed at our staff meeting, and I write that down. Keeping notes helps me pay attention to the details that make our program successful.

I don't look to find fault. I'm only interested in us correcting our mistakes and getting better. So that notecard goes with me into the next morning's staff meeting. And be assured that during the next day's practice, I'll be looking to see if we manage to get the problem corrected. During a game, that notecard will have some issues I want addressed at halftime, and other issues that will be addressed at the staff meeting on Monday morning.

Notecards are my primary evaluation tool. I don't need written performance evaluations. If someone's not doing his job, I'll notice it on the practice field or during a game.

✳

You might expect me to say that wins and losses are my ultimate criteria for evaluating performance. After all, how we perform on game day is the bottom line.

But it really isn't the bottom line for me.

If winning is the ultimate criterion, then I've put the cart before the horse. No matter how badly I want to win, I realize that an undue emphasis on winning will skew everything. It will skew our moral values, which take priority over winning. It will skew our faith, which recognizes that life is bigger than football. And it will require me to evaluate my staff in ways I'm not willing to do.

We will never take a win-at-all-costs approach in this program.

If we devise a good plan, and if good people work diligently to execute that plan within the framework of my philosophy, WINNING WILL TAKE CARE OF ITSELF.

If it happens that my philosophy causes us to lose, then maybe God has some other plan for my life.

✳

I persistently remind my coaches not to let an undependable guy play on the first team just because he has great ability. He will let you down at a critical moment.

I made this mistake in 1974 and nearly got fired for it. I made a coach keep a player on the first team when I knew his dependability was below average. This kid was muscular from head to toe, with a perfectly cut waist and a bulging chest. Yet he cost us several games because he didn't know what he was doing out there on the field. Why didn't he know? Because he skipped too many practices with lame excuses, and then didn't practice hard when he did show up. I was just so impressed with his physical skills that I couldn't cut him loose. The kid wasn't coachable, and he cost us some games.

I haven't made that mistake again.

When the pro scouts came around that year, they noticed him on the field and asked why I didn't put his name on the list of players for them to observe. *My goodness*, they said to me, *this guy's got more physical tools and is a better-crafted physical specimen than anyone else on your team. Why didn't you put us on to him?*

My answer was simple: They would be wasting time and money on this kid. He couldn't be counted on to do what they asked at the professional level.

If a person is undependable, you are foolish to put yourself in a position where you must depend on him to get your job done.

An undependable player is one who is frequently late to meetings, who misses practices, and who always has an excuse for his sub-par performance on the field. He is always hurt on Tuesday – our hardest workday during the regular season – and yet by Friday is in prime condition for the game.

I won't let that guy get me beat. He'll watch the game from the sidelines until he's healthy enough to practice on Tuesdays. If he never manages to get healthy on Tuesdays, I'll dismiss him from the team.

I don't mean to sound harsh, but I think I have a fair grasp of human nature. Some people will be as lazy as you allow them to be. Stern measures may be the only way to reform them. When a mother eagle is pregnant, she builds an aerie high up on the ledge of a cliff. There she births and nurtures her young hatchlings. When the mother decides they've lived long enough in the nest, she lifts them up with her beak and drops them over the edge. It's a long way down. Those who wish to fly have a golden opportunity to learn. The lazy ones are in for a big surprise.

Sometimes I have to play the role of "Eagle Bowden."

14
METING OUT DISCIPLINE

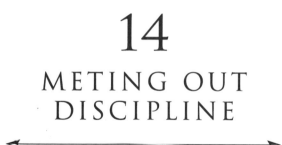

I prefer to lead with a baton rather than a big stick.

I started out my career as a strident disciplinarian. It was short hair, "yes, sir" and "no, sir," no tattoos, no earrings, and absolutely no disrespect toward the coaches. Definitely my way or the highway. Any player who challenged my rules was dismissed from the team. And any coach who divorced or drank alcoholic beverages or used drugs could not be kept on the staff. I was a child of my times who also happened to have a strong religious upbringing. Many of my expectations, especially regarding player discipline, were typical of that era.

As I passed through my 40s, 50s, and 60s, and now during my 70s, I have eased up somewhat, except in regard to morality and my personal ideals. Someone once said that if you hold a bird in your hand too tightly, you will kill it, but if you hold it too loosely, it will get away. I squeezed a little too tightly in my younger years.

＊

The biggest mistake made today with the modern athlete is not explaining to the player why he must do something and how it will benefit him. If you explain it to him, he will comply.

＊

My rulebook contains several non-negotiables that should not be transgressed.

Drug abuse, academic negligence, dissention, stealing, lying, and major crime will get a player kicked off the team.

Laziness, cheating, immorality, and illegal activity will get a coach dismissed.

＊

Back when I was an assistant coach at West Virginia in the 1960s, I learned a very important lesson from head coach Jim Carlen:

DON'T HAVE TOO MANY RULES. HAVE AS FEW AS YOU POSSIBLY CAN, BUT ENFORCE THEM.

＊

My coaches will get on a player pretty hard during practice if the player misses an assignment or hasn't paid attention to instructions. But when it comes to disciplinary matters, I want those situations handled confidentially.

During practice, I might notice that a player's hair is too long to suit me. Instead of calling out his name in front of the whole team and saying *Get it cut*, I'll sidle up to him during practice and whisper, *John, you need shorter hair. Get it done by tomorrow.*

If his hair is uncut when he comes to practice the next day, I'll call him over to me and say, *John, if your hair isn't cut by tomorrow, I'll run you after practice until your tongue hangs out.*

If he still hasn't responded by the third day, I'll tell him to go turn in his uniform. He's through playing for me.

＊

I try to think the best of people. They may prove me wrong, but I'll begin by giving them the benefit of the doubt. This has saved me on numerous occasions from foolishly and erroneously rushing to judgment.

＊

The biggest disciplinary mistake I've made during my career, and I've made it more than once, is waiting too long before kicking a player off my team. My reluctance has nothing to do with winning games. I just hate to give up on a kid if there's some way to help him improve his life.

I'm not thinking here of the player who commits a major crime or fails a drug test or physically abuses his girlfriend. Those boys are automatically dismissed. I'm thinking, rather, of the 1,001 problems you have with almost any boy between the ages of 18 and 22. A number of my players over the years have come from impoverished backgrounds with little or no parental influence and little exposure to religion. They weren't raised like I was. And they sometimes struggle to fit into my system and abide by my rules. Some overtly rebel against authority, reminding me of a bronco that's being broken for the saddle. Sending those kids back into the neighborhood is sometimes the easiest and most uncaring thing a coach can do. I'll stick with a player as long as I can. We coaches will discipline him internally.

Kicking a boy off the team is a very popular thing to do. The public loves such "heroic action" by a coach. They can say, *Look how tough our coach is.* But it's often the wrong thing to do. Defending a player is very unpopular at times. But I don't mind being unpopular, if that's the consequence of caring for my players.

I was more rigid in my younger years. I'm just not that way any more.

✳

I refuse to criticize or embarrass my coaches in front of the players. I've known some popular coaches who openly demeaned their assistant coaches right there on the practice field, and I think it's deplorable.

Let me cite a few reasons for my position.

First and foremost, I wouldn't want to be treated that way by my superior. If I was an assistant coach, I'd want my boss to meet with me in private to discuss any differences might we have. I owe the same treatment to my staff.

Second, the coach who has just been belittled in front of his players has now lost a measure of credibility with them. I need my players to respect and obey their position coach. Criticism only robs the coach of credibility in front of the very people he must train, motivate, and hold accountable. How does belittling him help my cause? It doesn't. In fact, it creates more problems for me. I don't want players thinking they can squabble and argue with the coach over every little thing they don't like. And don't think for a minute that football players are any different from anyone else in this regard. A few of them will try to take advantage of any apparent dissention within the coaching ranks. It's human nature to do so. I simply refuse to saddle myself with those kinds of added problems.

Third, open criticism sends a dangerous message to my players — namely, that I don't really have much respect for the very men I've hired to help run the program. I don't want our football program looking like some Mickey Mouse operation riddled with internal strife.

If criticism is in order, I will wait until the next staff meeting to address the problem. Of course, if it's a serious problem or one that cannot wait until later, then I'll call the coach aside or get him alone in a private conversation.

* * *

I've learned better than to embarrass a coach in front of his fellow coaches.

Some leaders think nothing of getting the staff together and then unloading on one of them in front of the others. This is a foolish, foolish action. It hurts morale. It leaves staff members afraid to make independent decisions. It makes people burn with a slow, hidden anger. And it destroys the bonds of trust and loyalty so necessary to good leadership.

I will never back down from addressing a problem with a member of my staff. Heck, my job depends on those guys. I don't want them doing things that might cause us to lose ballgames or cause me to get fired. I want them doing what I've asked them to do. But "beating up" on someone in front of his peers isn't a good way to mete out discipline. Such imprudence compounds a problem rather than resolving it.

I won't go into a staff meeting and say to a coach, *Look, I told you yesterday how I want you to coach those blocking techniques. Why can't you just do what I told you to do?*

I also won't pretend to mask my criticism by saying, *Look, coach, I'm not trying to beat you up or embarrass you on this issue, but why in the world can't you do what I asked you to do?*

Aren't both of these statements really saying the same thing? Haven't I just beat him up and embarrassed him despite my disclaimer?

If I must be direct with a coach during a staff meeting, I still try to get my point across indirectly. I might ask, *Coach, what were you trying to accomplish yesterday in practice when you did such-and-such?* It's a fair question, and I ask it sincerely. Maybe the coach has a good reason for doing what he did, even if it wasn't what I wanted done. Perhaps his players couldn't work on the blocking scheme because they still needed work on their take-off steps. I won't know unless I ask. If the answer I get is not satisfactory, then I can reiterate that today I want the players to work on blocking schemes. The conversation might conclude with me saying, *Well, we do need those take-off steps to be correct. You're right about that. But today, no doubt about it, the players must get a solid 30 minutes of work on those blocking schemes. Do you know of anything that would prevent us from getting that work done?* That's about as much as I might say on the subject in a staff meeting.

If the problem persists, we will discuss it in the privacy of my office.

I much prefer to be indirect when it comes to disciplining a staff member in front of his peers. I may learn that a coach has not been visiting all the high school games like he was supposed to. My most common reaction is to issue a warning to the entire staff. I'll say, *Men, be sure you cover all your high school games. Someone called and said one of you has not been by. Let's don't let that happen anymore.* The coach gets the message. And anyone else who might have missed some games will think I'm talking about him.

I once used this indirect method to reprimand a single staff member, and three coaches came into my office that afternoon to apologize!

If I notice dissention between two of my coaches, I will ask them to come into my office together. When they sit down, I'll lean over my desk and say, *Men, what's the problem? I don't think you two guys like each other. I can't have dissention on my staff. So which of you wants to leave?* Then they'll tell me their problem and I'll solve it for them. I might simply tell them to work together and hide any animosity they may feel. But they understand that no more overt dissention is allowed.

✳

I rarely face a disciplinary issue with members of my staff. If you hire the right people, you don't have discipline problems. My staff does it right or they get fired.

That's understood.

✳

When I think of disciplining my players, one memory stands out more clearly than all others, and it has influenced my method for 50 years.

It was my senior year in college and our last game of the season. A number of my teammates had decided the night before to stay out late and have some fun before the big game on Saturday. The next day, prior to the game, our head coach found out that his curfew rules had been broken. So he refused to let any of them play in the final game of their careers.

It was also the final game for others of us who didn't violate curfew.

I quarterbacked our team to a totally unnecessary defeat in that last game of my collegiate career. We didn't have a chance to win with so many of our key players out of the line-up. To no one's surprise, we got smeared.

I was disappointed in our coach because he hurt the entire team with his method of punishment. I'm still disappointed 50 years later. There were any number of ways he could've punished those guys without punishing the rest of us as well. I mean, all these fellows did was stay out later than the coach said they could stay out. It wasn't as if they shot the president. Maybe when I get to heaven, God will prove wiser than my coach and allow us all to play that last game one more time.

To this day, unless conditions absolutely dictate otherwise, I will not cause the entire team to suffer because of the foolishness of one or two players. There are many ways to punish a player. I can make him run stadium steps at 5 A.M. or run gassers after practice.

I can take away his monthly *per diem*, or take away his meal privileges, or kick him out of the dorm and let him find his own place to sleep. The player will probably prefer to sit out a game, but I don't ask for his opinion.

I've dismissed a lot of players from my team over the years. And many players have been forced to sit out of one or more games because of misconduct. But I will deny game privileges to a player only if the punishment fits the crime. Public sentiment will have absolutely no bearing on my decision.

Some fans and sportswriters think that by allowing an offending player to play in a game, I have demonstrated a lack of backbone. I just remember my senior year in college, and the last game of my career. What my coach did wasn't fair to me or to the rest of my team. I refuse to repeat his mistake.

※

Back when I first began coaching, if a player got into trouble, the problem was resolved by the coach, the player, and a third party (a professor, a law enforcement officer, a property owner, and so forth). I always made the player apologize to the victim, and then I punished the player for what he did.

I did not make any public announcements about what the player had done or how I had punished him. To me, it was none of the public's business. My attitude was, and still remains, "I'll handle it."

Now everyone wants to play the disciplinary game. A player gets disorderly in public, and the press puts his picture on the front of the sports page. By the next day, the story makes national news. Then it takes on a life of its own. The public gets involved. The school president gets involved. The administrative staff gets involved. And suddenly the worst of all possible solutions occurs: discipline by committee. And the committee of judges is usually made up of people who can't handle the heat.

I try to cut those folks out of the loop whenever I can.

I know how to handle the situation.

Corrective discipline will not be overlooked.

15
MORALE

←—————————————————————→

High morale may be the greatest advantage
you can bring into a game.

When I first arrived in Tallahassee, my new staff and I met hour upon hour throughout the month of January, laying the framework of the program we would install at Florida State. Each of us pledged to work within this framework and win or lose with these fundamentals. At the heart of our new program was the notion of TEAM FIRST.[i]

The team was bigger than any individual and had top priority. The team included everyone involved with the program, from coaches and players to trainers and managers. Everyone had a role to fulfill. No matter how difficult the days might be, or how grueling the work, or how great our adversities, we had to put TEAM ahead of ourselves.

I heard about the Total Quality Management approach when it was so popular back in the 1980s. I don't know if that stuff is

---

[i] *Bound for Glory*, by Bobby Bowden as told to Mike Bynum, The *We Believe* Trust Fund, College Station, TX, 1980, p.138.

still popular today because I don't keep up with trendy fashions. I just use common sense. But there is some similarity between TQM and my own style in regard to the team approach. I don't go out and create teams to solve problems in my organization, but I do recognize that we're all in it together and we'll sink or swim together.

This TEAM concept is the key to our morale. We have great morale at FSU because coaches and players are regularly reminded, and shown, how their best efforts work to make the team better.

In staff meetings and at our annual hideaway meeting, I repeat this message to my coaches. I DEMAND good morale from them. Coaches are the absolute key to high morale among our players. Any coach who does not believe he can contribute to high morale will not be retained on my staff. Good morale among the players is coachable. I know it is because we've done it here at Florida State for 25 years.

I get involved with the players myself in the morale-building process.

Before every practice, I call our players together to tell them how today's practice will make them better – and how it will benefit them – if they give their best effort every minute of that day. The walk-ons no less than the scholarship athletes, and the back-ups as well as the starters, must do their part and make their valuable contribution to the success of that day's practice.

The result is consistently good morale.

My job is to make sure we maintain it.

＊

Let me share with you some observations I've made about morale.

First, creating good morale does not require a warm, bubbly personality or the ingenuity of Sigmund Freud. If it did, I'd be dead in the water. That just isn't me.

I'm a coach, not a cheerleader or a *rah-rah* kind of guy. My top priority is to ensure that we all do our jobs. When I hire coaches, I expect them to do the job they're being paid for. When I recruit players, I expect them to play up to their level of ability. Every once in a while, we need to make attitude adjustments. But for the most part, I try to do my job, and I expect the same from others.

Second, I don't consider it my job to make everyone happy.

Having good morale doesn't mean that my staff members and players act like happy-go-lucky pollyannas. Good morale *can* mean happiness, of course, but it means other things, too, that are unrelated to a momentary good feeling.

Good morale can mean being focused on winning a game. It can mean being well prepared or determined to perform better on the practice field. It can mean committing yourself to be more disciplined with your studies or your weight-room training. It can mean resolving not to make mountains out of molehills. All of these are indicators of good morale. None of them are necessarily related to happiness.

Third, good morale doesn't mean that people are content with their jobs.

In my profession, someone is always unhappy about something. Our players absolutely do not like our winter conditioning drills. And they hate going into August practices when the temperature hovers around 100 degrees. The third teamers don't like to sit on the bench during games. The second-string quarterback is never content with second best. The walk-ons would much rather have earned a scholarship. On and on I could go. Can you imagine how ridiculous it would be for me to call a team meeting and say, *Okay, guys, my top priority is for you to be content with your current situation.* That won't happen as long as I'm coaching. I want that second-string quarterback pushing for a starting job. I want that walk-on linebacker to teach these scholarship boys a thing or two about determination. The drive for improvement is born of dissatisfaction. And sometimes (excuse the mixed metaphor) the head coach has to stir the pot. You might call it *positive agitation.*

If good morale meant contentment, I would've failed at my job long ago. You simply cannot make everyone happy or give them what they believe they deserve. Grumbling will happen. Some will walk off and quit the team. I've learned to accept a measure of discontent as the cost of doing business. Heck, if a player will quit over a slight discontentment, he probably would've quit down in the trenches during a game when things got tough.

Good morale means that we have a healthy, positive environment in which to do our jobs. And it means that everyone believes his job is important. It DOES NOT MEAN they all get what they want.

✳

Here are some particular things I do to build and maintain good morale:

1. First and foremost, religious faith is put squarely in the center of our professional lives. Nothing does more to maintain high morale than a positive faith in God.

We coaches bring our faith to work. We make a place for faith at work. People can say what they want about keeping God out of the workplace. Maybe those folks are smarter than the God they want to replace. Maybe they know a better way to help people deal with the complexities of life. But I've been around a long time. And here's all I'll say in defense of my pro-religion stance:

Let me tell you sometime about all the problems I DON'T HAVE in my organization because our top commitment is to God, not to football.

We've held staff meeting devotionals since 1987, and I've seen the change it's made for us. We won't reverse directions now.

Our players and coaches pray together before and after ballgames. Our players are encouraged to join the local Fellowship of Christian Athletes or some other campus religious organization of their choosing. I write the parents of all our athletes and ask permission to take their son to church twice a year with the team. In 50 years of coaching, only one parent has denied permission. We have a team chaplain who counsels our players. And many of our players meet with opposing players after each ballgame to have prayer in the middle of the field.

Do you really want to build positive morale in your organization? If so, then when you open for business, invite God in.

2. I delegate responsibilities to my staff members, then give them the authority to carry out their responsibilities and make decisions on their own. They don't have to come and ask for my approval on many matters that I've entrusted to them. They know how my program should be run, and they enjoy being treated like the responsible professionals they are.

3. As I've said before, I encourage my staff to be independent thinkers, to express their opinions freely, and to openly disagree with me or with one another, provided that two conditions are met: (i) arguing must be done in a constructive spirit as a means to help us improve, and (ii) arguing must be done during a staff meeting (or in the privacy of the coaches' office) and may not be taken outside the room.

4. I always support my coaches in a dispute. I tell my players, *Don't talk back to your coach. If you do, I'll back the coach.* Players can come to me, if they wish, and I will listen to them. I might agree with them and work to make corrections. But I want my coaches to see that I will support them if they are doing their job.

5. I will not criticize my coaches in front of a player or in any public venue. I also will not criticize my players in the media.

6. I ask my coaches not to make any derogatory statements about one another in front of players or in any other public venue.

7. I will not fly off the handle and vent my momentary frustration on a coach or player. I've heard people excuse their own brash behavior by saying, *Sure, I fly off the handle every once in a while, but then I'm over it quickly. That's just the way I am.* Well, atomic bombs don't last long either, but the long-term damage is tremendous. *Ready, shoot, aim* is not a formula for good staff morale.

8. We coaches take the time to explain to players why we make certain demands and follow certain procedures. We try to show how they can become better football players, perhaps become an All-American or an NFL prospect. We also try to show how certain virtues demanded of football will also help them succeed in life.

People who think that coaches berate players mercilessly, or drive them like cattle and use them only as means to our personal ends, don't understand human nature and don't understand today's athletes. Modern football players would never stand for such behavior from coaches. They would quit on us, either by walking off the team or refusing to give their best. Good coaching requires us to make intense demands while building morale, team spirit, and an appreciation of the value of disciplined effort.

9. I will call selected seniors together when necessary and challenge them to lead the team. If we don't have good senior leadership, we're in trouble. The seniors are older and wiser. Their younger teammates will listen to them.

✳

People will work hard and fight tenaciously when properly motivated. Underdogs will fight more fiercely than anyone.

I learned this lesson my junior year in high school, when I was the starting quarterback at Woodlawn High School in Birmingham, Alabama.

My coach, Kenny Morgan, called me into his office after practice one day. We had a big game coming up that Friday night. Coach Morgan wanted to share a rumor he'd heard. The opposing coach, he told me, was saying that I was not playing up to my potential, and that their players would "put me out of the game."

By the time I left Coach Morgan's office, I was hopping mad and all fired up to play. Nobody was going to knock me out of a game.

On game day, during our warm-up exercises on the field, I gave that opposing coach the meanest glare I could muster. I resolved to show them all how tough I could be. And when the game started, I went out and kicked their tail.

Later, I discovered that Coach Morgan made up the story to motivate me.

The experience taught me a valuable lesson about the power of motivation. Since then, and during my entire coaching career, I've looked for little ways to keep coaches and players motivated to do their best. Motivated people are tough to beat.

✳

Morale is different from enthusiasm.

Enthusiasm is more of an occasional phenomenon. Some people are enthusiastic almost all the time. But most people need to be pumped up. Fiery speeches, inspiring stories, direct challenges, and satisfying rewards are the stuff used to generate enthusiasm.

Morale is more of a day-in-and-day-out phenomenon. If team morale is good all week, our players will be amply prepared and motivated for the game on Saturday. But if morale is sagging, my coaches and I must find ways to pump them up and generate some enthusiasm.

16
SALARIES AND PROMOTIONS

*I've never found a connection between salary
level and job performance.*

Few issues are more important to staff members than salaries and promotions. It's understandable. Salaries pay the bills. Promotions prepare assistant coaches for head coaching jobs.

You may never hear your employees discussing their remuneration. But be assured they are discussing it at home. When I was coming up in the profession, my wife never felt I was compensated adequately. I didn't think so, either, but she helped to keep my memory fresh. I think she reminded me almost every payday that I was worth more than I was being paid.

Most people are very sensitive about salary-related issues – and rarely more so than in coaching. Few coaches make large salaries. Many will scrape by each year to make ends meet. And on top of that, a few mediocre seasons can get a coach fired. You learn to gather your rosebuds while you may.

Promotion issues are no less thorny. It's not just the dilemma of promoting one person ahead of another. It's also the fact that many professions have windows of opportunity for advancement. At one stage in life, you're too young to ask for a promotion. At another stage, you're too old to expect it. When a head coach makes promotions, he is influencing the careers of several people at the same time.

A wise leader will treat these two issues with utmost seriousness.

✳

I never make jokes about a coach's salary or about anything related to promotions.

Never.

Ever.

Sometimes a boss is just trying to be funny when he says to an employee, *I guess I'll just have to stop paying you so much money* or *I'll just have to cut your pay for that.* The employee will laugh outwardly, but he doesn't really find it funny. In fact, he may find it offensive that you make such a sensitive issue the butt of a joke.

Some issues are just better left alone, no matter how much you think your employees like you or how innocent your comment is intended to be.

Salaries and promotions are not joking matters.

✳

A job represents the chance to do something important in life. The paycheck is important, of course, because it pays the bills. People need a livable wage. But people who enjoy their jobs aren't in it for the money. Provided with the proper motivation, they'll do what it takes to make ends meet.

I got into coaching because I loved the challenge of the game. The men who coached me – particularly Kenny Morgan, my high school football coach – had my deepest respect and admiration. I wanted to be part of their great fraternity. So I chased the dream, knowing that economic hardship came with the territory. Living under financial strain was difficult, but I loved my job more than I hated my empty wallet.

I think most workers share my sentiment. And a leader who has responsibility for determining salaries or wages should keep this in mind. Properly motivated people will work hard to do a good job, even if they don't earn as much as they'd like.

When I started out in coaching at South Georgia College in 1955, my annual salary was $4,600. With three children, and a fourth on the way, I needed more money. So I worked extra jobs during the summer months. The summer days were occupied with life-guard duty at the college's swimming pool from 10 A.M. until 5 P.M. At nights, I worked the 8 P.M. - 8 A.M. graveyard shift at a local tobacco warehouse. I caught sleep whenever I could.

At the warehouse, I unloaded big bales of tobacco brought in each evening by delivery trucks. Things often slowed down around 2:00 A.M. Whenever possible, I'd climb on top of a tall stack of tobacco leaves and sleep a few hours during the night. Big brown rats nested in those tobacco leaves. They never let me sleep very long. There's nothing quite like waking up eyeball-to-eyeball with a 12-inch rat.

During the Christmas season, my wife Ann worked at the Sears mail-order store while I delivered mail for the local post office. The post office would fill a big metal wagon with mail for delivery to local businesses. And like a horse in harness, the athletic director and head football coach of South Georgia College could be seen pulling his wagonload of envelopes and packages down Main Street each day. The road was made of cobbled brick, and the wagon sometimes got stuck in the cracks. I'm not making this up. We had bills to pay.

Ann and I also served as resident assistants in one of the school dormitories, which helped us save on rent. Ann mended the children's clothes and passed them down from one child to the next. I bought barber shears and gave my boys haircuts. Somehow, we managed to make ends meet.

Four years passed. We left Georgia and moved to Alabama for another four years. The family grew to six children. Money was still tight. We moved on to Florida for three years, then up to West Virginia for another 10 years. Still not enough money. I continued struggling to keep my nose above the waterline all through the first half of my career. Not until the mid-1980s did I finally feel I was making some economic headway. By that time, my children were grown and gone.

I understand why salary is a sensitive issue. More than just egos are at stake when it comes to getting paid.

＊

I've always believed in paying my top assistants a higher salary than the others. If you lose a good coordinator, he will be hard to replace. The other coaching positions can be filled more easily.

＊

I'm given a budget each year by the athletic director. That budget indicates how much money is provided for coaches' salaries and raises in the upcoming fiscal year. The budget, for instance, might include an extra $50,000 for raises. I normally take that lump-sum amount and give all assistant coaches an equal percentage increase in pay. The dollar amounts will be different for each coach, of course, since the higher-paid coach gets more money than the lower-paid coach. But at least I can say that everyone received the same percentage increase.

There are occasions, however, when I decide to give my coordinators a larger raise than the others. If the coordinator is a candidate for a higher-paying job, and if I feel he fits better than anyone else into my plans for our program, then the coordinator will get a larger share of my available money.

I can never make everyone happy, and I regret that.

But everyone knows what his salary will be before taking a job on my staff. If a coach doesn't want the job, I'll give it to someone else. And if he can make more money working somewhere else, I won't oppose his effort to improve himself.

＊

I'd like for every coach to be convinced that he is receiving a fair and livable wage. In fact, I'd like them all to have enough discretionary income that they can enjoy leisure activities and perhaps afford a few more material comforts.

But I also know something else. There's no cause-effect relationship between salary and work performance. Doubling a person's salary does not guarantee that he will thereby perform twice as well, or even perform any better than the previous year.

＊

I have three pieces of advice for anyone who must deal with issues of salary and promotion.

First and most important, when you are hiring someone, painting a darker picture is better than painting a lighter picture. Don't miss the opportunity to solve certain problems before they ever arise.

By dark, I mean realistic. Here's what I might say to a coach I'm about to hire:

Coach Smith, here's what the job pays. And based on my past experience, here's what you're likely to receive in raises each year. Whatever it is, I'll expect you to accept it without complaint, because I'm doing the best I know to do. If you think your salary level will be a problem in the future, you'd be wise to decide now if you really want the job.

Sometimes, on top of cost-of-living increases, the university will give me some additional money to pass out in raises to my staff. My preference is to share this money equally with all my coaches. But don't assume that I'll do that, because I may not. I may give more to the coordinators if I feel it's necessary to keep them here. I don't want hurt feelings as a result.

I also want you to know that I prefer to promote from within rather than going outside my program for a new coach. When that time comes, I'll choose the person who best fits with my plans at that time. The person who gets promoted may not be the most popular coach among the staff, or the one who's been here the longest. He'll be the one I believe best fits within my larger strategy for our program. Several staff members will want the job. You may be one of them, and I may not pick you. But if that happens, it doesn't mean that I question your ability or am unhappy with your performance. I want you to understand what I'm saying, because I do not tolerate dissention on my staff.

You do yourself and your organization a huge favor if you practice preventative medicine during the interview process. Many future problems can be eliminated or downgraded if you deal with them on the front end

Second, do not create expectations that you cannot fulfill.

You may be so excited to hire a great prospect that you paint a bright picture of his future. But you don't control the future. It's not yours to promise. Your eagerness to hire someone, or your own dreams for your organization's future success, could entice you to fill this person with all sorts of unreasonable hopes. The fellow sitting across from you will remember every word you say to him. So be cautious. Be realistic. Paint with darker colors. You have a teachable moment. Use it wisely.

Third, when necessary, I explain my salary or promotion decision to the coaches involved. If three of my coaches want a coordinator's position and only one gets it, I have two guys with hurt feelings. That's going to happen because the other two believe they are qualified for the job. I'll meet with them individually and explain my decision. Maybe one's too young and just isn't ready for the added responsibility. I can tell him in so many words, without hurting his feelings, that he's not ready for such consideration at this point. But maybe the other coach *is* qualified but still got passed over. That's a more difficult situation, and I owe him some insight into my thinking. My words must be carefully chosen, not for my sake, but for his. He wouldn't be on my staff if he was doing a poor job. In our conversation, I will not question his ability (e.g., *I didn't promote you because you lack . . .*) or criticize his personal skills (e.g., *The other guy just gets along so well with our coaches . . .*). I might say simply:

I made the decision that best fit within my plans. The guy who got the job might not fit best in another position that comes available. Maybe you fit best there, but that position isn't open now. I see each of my coaches fitting best into certain roles, according to what works best for our program, but those other positions may not come open anytime soon, and they may never come open. I don't divulge my future plans until there is a need to know. But I try to determine, in each situation, which pieces should go where.

Then I'll remind him that I'm pleased with his work and hope he'll be with us for a long time.

That's about the best I know to do.

I never got a single job I applied for, including a coordinator's job I wanted back early in my career. Some things a person just has to accept. And if he cannot accept them, then he needs to move on.

✳

If workers cannot be rewarded with as much money as they want, look for other ways to reward them. I said earlier that a job represents an opportunity to do something important in life. Well, are your employees made to feel their importance? Is the value of their work made known to them and others?

I try to showcase my staff as often as possible when I do media interviews or speak to booster groups. Why not? If they do good work, someone other than me ought to know about it. So when a coach does a noteworthy job, I make a habit of expressing my appreciation in some public venue.

I figure they'd swap these newspaper highlights for an increase in pay, but I can't always provide the pay raise.

People aren't machines. You pay $1000 for a machine and then expect it to do its job without complaint or expectation. People, in contrast, have hopes and aspirations. They long for a satisfying life. While it's true that we should expect an honest day's work for an honest day's pay, people simply can't be treated like machines.

Every person who works for you wants to live a life worth dying for. In fact, that's what we all want – namely, to get to the end of our days and look back with satisfaction. Work is a big part of life. In fact, work may be the most defining feature of our individual life stories.

One of the most frequently asked questions of new acquaintances is, *What do you do for a living?* The question speaks volumes about the close relationship between working and living.

Good leadership sometimes shows itself in the ability to transform a job into a meaningful journey.

17
CONFIDENTIALITY

$$\longleftrightarrow$$

Nothing wins admiration and respect like the ability
to keep confidences.

Leaders are privy to a lot of confidential information, particularly relating to other members of the organization. Most of this information should not be shared with any subordinates. The ability to keep matters in confidence is one of the best signs of a good leader.

But keeping secrets is difficult.

Some employees live to learn secrets. They'll pry and cajole for all the secret office tidbits they can get. Others can't wait to share the latest inside information they've heard. Secret news is juicy news, and telling it is absolutely delicious. Plus, one's value appears to increase in direct proportion to the knowledge acquired. It's an adult version of the childhood taunt *I know something you don't know.*

Leaders must not play this game. Like a black hole that absorbs light but lets none escape, the good leader will keep things to himself.

Leaders who cannot keep confidences violate a fundamental tenet of the leadership covenant: Secrets always flow up, never down or sideways.

✳

Leaders learn things they have no business repeating to anyone in their organization. And leaders are told things they know should be kept private. Maybe the employee who shares a confidence with you hasn't really said that he wants you to keep it a secret. But you know the conversation should be kept confidential because you would want the same thing kept secret about you.

Doctors, lawyers, and ministers are pretty good about keeping confidences. Their jobs depend on it. I'd hate to spill my guts to some minister, only to discover that he tells his wife everything he learns at the office.

My wife sometimes accuses me of being tight-lipped about work. I am. I'm good at keeping a secret. I got good by making confidentiality a behavioral habit. After a while, maintaining confidentiality became easy. Heck, I still know things about my children that they think I don't know.

If you can manage to keep things to yourself, even when the person probably wouldn't mind if you told others, you'll stand taller than the Jolly Green Giant in their eyes.

I admire anyone with the strength of character to keep his mouth shut out of respect for another person.

✳

There are some occasions when I will share personal information. If I learn that Coach Smith is having problems with his oldest son, I might mention this to the other coaches and say, *Let's try to help him.* The disclosure must be for a constructive purpose that requires some action by those who have been told. Of course, if I learned about it from Coach Smith himself, who asked me to keep it between us, then I would respect his request for confidentiality.

✳

Rarely will a player ever share a confidence with me. A few will, but most won't. I think they view me as too far removed from their day-to-day world. Players are more likely to talk with the team chaplain or with their position coach. I'm very comfortable with this arrangement. Unless it's something I absolutely need to know about, it's fine with me for my staff to know things that I don't.

My assistant coaches, however, do sometimes share confidential information with me. Some of this information is very personal. Perhaps a coach feels that I need an explanation for his absence from a staff meeting or his failure to get something done. Or maybe he's got a problem with one of his coaching colleagues that he can't get resolved on his own. Whatever we discuss stays in my office. If the disclosure requires me to take action, I'll do it in a way that maintains the confidentiality covenant.

✳

Two things happen when you don't keep confidences at work. Both of them are bad.

First, you lose the trust of other people. Let's say an employee tells you something that might prove embarrassing to him, or that would demean him if it became public knowledge, and you cannot resist the temptation to share this conversation with another colleague. So maybe you tell the vice-president, who is also your friend and next-door neighbor. Of course, in your own unique way, you warn him it's a secret that shouldn't be repeated. Then you tell him. The vice-president now feels special. You've made him your confidant. But the vice-president also learns something about you – namely, that you're the kind of person who can't keep a secret. At some point he'll begin thinking, *O Lord, what information have I shared with this guy that I hoped wouldn't be repeated?* And that's coming from the one person in the office you're closest to. If the victim of your indiscretion ever finds out, you also will have made an enemy.

Second, failure to keep confidences can create dissention in the ranks. If you tell my colleague something I assumed you would keep in confidence, I now feel awkward around both of you. I resent *you* for telling and *him* for knowing. I'm inclined now to smear your reputation among the people I work with, because you have secret information that can embarrass me.

Do you really want that kind of work environment?

✳

If someone divulges information that you feel compelled to share with another person, then do one of two things: either ask for permission to share the information – which is the best course of action – or tell the person why you must share it and to whom you will talk. Choose the latter course only when failure to do so will have dire consequences.

✳

I've developed one habit that really helps me guard against violating a confidence: I always try to say only good things about other people. It may sound simple, but it works well, and in more ways than one.

The few times I have popped off and said something critical of a person, it came back to bite me.

✳

In all the years I've been in coaching, the biggest and most unfortunate shift to occur in athletics is the shift away from privacy and confidentiality toward the direction of full public disclosure.

Nothing is confidential anymore. This is wrong. And most of the blame rests with the news media.

When your child disobeys you, you punish the child, but you don't go out and announce it to the neighborhood. How would that help anyone? Some things just don't need to go outside the family.

When I was playing ball back in the late 1940s, if a player got into trouble, someone might call his coach, and the coach would handle it. Maybe the kid was cutting class and the professor called the coach. The coach would run that boy after practice until his tongue was hanging out, then he'd check the boy's attendance record for the rest of the semester. Or if a player was arrested for drinking or disorderly conduct, the sheriff might call the coach to come get him, and the coach might kick the player out of the dorm for one semester, take away his meal money, or even take his scholarship away for a year. The coach could hit the boy where it hurt. Goodness, when I was at South Georgia College, I received more than one of those calls. And you can be assured that the player not only was disciplined but also was monitored to guard against relapses. Relapses would get a kid kicked off the team.

That's how I was raised, and that's still the way I prefer to treat my players. If they do something wrong I will discipline them, but it will remain between them and me, or maybe between them and the legal system. Why heap additional shame upon the player and his family?

It ain't that way anymore, if the news media can help it.

Certain members of the press now check police files every morning to see who was arrested the night before. If a football player's name happens to show up, that player's name will be broadcast all over the radio and TV before I wake up in the morning. Then I read about it again when I open the sports page. Now I have the general public, the school administration, and the entire university on my case. This kind of thing really peeves me. I have no interest in fighting with the media, but this shameless disregard for privacy is one of the most distasteful things I've witnessed over the past 25 years. Sometimes it takes all my strength to refrain from telling a reporter, *It's none of your #!@# business!*

I will not volunteer information about player discipline to anyone outside of my program. If it's something the athletic director or university president needs to know, I'll certainly tell them. If it's a serious legal issue, then obviously it's out of my hands. But otherwise I will keep it in-house and deal with it behind closed doors.

I made the mistake two years ago of telling reporters at the Sugar Bowl that three of our players had missed curfew the night before.

I figured they'd find out sooner or later, so why not be nice and tell them myself? We've all had children who came home later than they were supposed to. You punish them and move on. Anyway, the players had broken a team rule, not a school policy or a law.

My disclosure to the press was a colossal mistake.

For the next few days leading up to the national championship game, all we heard about was how inexcusably I was handling the punishment of one of these three offenders. The player in question was Sebastian Janikowski, a Polish immigrant who also was our All-American place-kicker. I had decided to let him start the game, while the other two players had to sit out the first few plays. Well, when the media came back the next day and grilled me about my decision, I responded by making a joke. I told them that Janikowski was judged under international rules! I thought my quip was funny. All it did was make things worse.

The story was blown up to an incredible size. ESPN gave it national exposure. Even the play-by-play TV broadcasters made it a centerpiece story just prior to kickoff. Some painted it as an issue of integrity – or lack of integrity – for our program.

Here's what all that media attention accomplished. Leading up to the game, the players and coaches were distracted by endless questions about this single issue. The fans who paid vacation money to attend the game were treated to stories about their school's undisciplined football program. The university's opportunity for national exposure turned into a marketing catastrophe. And for what? For three kids who came in late one night (not from fighting or fleeing the scene of a crime) and a coaching staff who refused to divulge our punishment rationale to the general public.

Next time they'll have to find out on their own.

*

If the head coach is unhappy with a coach's performance, he should never discuss it with another staff member. As mentioned elsewhere in this book, I once worked for a guy who did that. He would pull one coach aside and criticize another coach on the staff. Or else he'd let it be known that he didn't like what old coach so-and-so is reported to have done. The target of his ire, of course, was never around when our boss expressed his opinions.

Maybe this was his way of getting word back to the coach in question. Whatever the intent, it's a sorry way to treat people.

At the very least, this behavior made him look bad. Was he afraid to deal with an issue head-on? If he's the man in charge, then why tell us about it? Why not just step in and do something?

He's the guy being paid to solve problems, not us. He had no right using us to do his dirty work. I didn't want to know his negative opinions about my coaching colleagues. And he had no right to share them. His tactics showed a lack of integrity.

The movie *Saving Private Ryan* had a great scene where Tom Hanks's character reminds a private in his unit that "*Gripes go up. They never go down.*" The private can gripe to the corporal, the corporal can gripe to the sergeant, and so on. Gripes go up the chain of command. They should never go down.

18

KEEPING A
PROFESSIONAL
DISTANCE

*Unless you've ever been there before, you don't realize
that it really is lonely at the top.*

I don't confide in, or share my personal life with, my staff members.

We aren't bosom buddies. We don't take vacations together. And I don't draw selected staff members into any kind of inner circle.

I keep my distance. Intentionally. There will be times when I must go against their wishes. They must accept that if I'm wrong, I'm still the boss.

It's not that I view my staff as men of inferior rank. That's not it at all. These are grown professionals that I work with, men of stature and proven skill. Some were head coaches before joining my staff. We don't have any insecurities that drive us into codependence.

Nonetheless, I recognize the need to maintain a professional distance. I wouldn't be their "best buddy" even if I wanted to. And I didn't expect differently when I was an assistant coach.

I once knew a business owner who had a young, growing company. He only had six employees at the time, and he insisted they all call him by his first name. His goal was to create a family atmosphere where they thought of him as their friend rather than as their boss. It's the typical mistake of a young leader, even though this fellow was in his early 40s.

The family atmosphere collapsed, however, the first time he had to deny someone a raise based on poor performance. Talk about internal strife. Things kept going downhill every time he exerted his authority or made an unpopular decision. A lot of his "family members" eventually quit and took other jobs. I'll wager they felt the way Esau did toward his brother Jacob after the birthright scandal: *I thought you were my friend. You knew how much I needed that raise, and you didn't give it to me. I feel betrayed.*

I love my staff members. I don't think I could have a better group of men to work with. They put up with me like I put up with them. But they aren't my family. If I want a family environment, I go on a family vacation. When I come into the office, I come into a work environment where I'm the head coach. There's a difference in the two environments, and I'm not about to get things confused.

✻

Seminaries teach young ministers this point before they ever head out to lead a congregation. If the minister wants a close friend, someone in whom he can confide or around whom he can just let his hair down, he is advised to find someone outside the congregation.

That's sage advice.

You can't choose sides within your organization when it comes to selecting a confidant or establishing an intimate friendship.

※

Keeping a professional distance means acting like a professional in all your dealings with staff and employees. You don't let your hair down in their presence.

As much as your employees may like you, they always are aware that you have an authority over them that they don't hold over you. They can't fire you, but you can fire them. They don't control your pay raises or bonuses or office hours or work responsibilities, but you control theirs.

This gulf separating you from them cannot be removed unless you choose to abdicate your role as leader. Until that happens, they will never talk as freely with you as they do among themselves. They'll always be more candid with their peers than they are with you. And they will withhold information from you that might cause problems if you knew.

That's the gulf.

It's there for a very good reason, and you shouldn't try to cross it.

Some leaders, however, just can't resist the temptation.

※

Unless you've ever been there before, you don't realize how lonely it can get at the top.

Sometimes I wish my staff could be here with me, such as when a tough decision must be made or when I long for the good old days of my youth as an assistant coach. Assistant coaches enjoy a camaraderie that doesn't include the boss.

I sometimes wish they could be here with me now.

But they can't.

✳

The politics of friendship work well in the political arena. You build coalitions with one group of voters and compete to outvote other coalitions of voters. Knowing you can never be the friend of all, you choose to be the friend of some. And you work hard to ensure that your coalition is the largest. Even after you get elected to represent all the different competing coalitions, your top priority is loyalty to the group that voted you into office. Let some Democratic president side too often with the Republicans in Congress, and he'll lose the next election. That's how politics works in this country, and it's worked passably well for over 200 years.

Just don't take this approach in your own organization, unless your employees have the right to vote you out as boss.

Leaders who try to build coalitions within their own organization will soon reduce the organization to a shambles. A leader may find himself thinking, *You know, if I befriend these two guys over here, they'll keep me apprised about what those two guys on the other side of the room are doing. Then I can stay on top of things in my organization.* Such a strategy will eventually work against you. I once worked for a head coach who tried to do that. Two things inevitably happen. Either the "friends of the boss" are looked upon as sniveling rats by the rest of us, or else they tell us what the boss is up to. In my case, it was the latter. None of us ended up respecting the guy. I left that job not long afterwards.

A wise leader understands that he must lead everyone equally and fairly. To accomplish this, he cannot show favoritism, bias, or allegiance to selected individuals.

*

The best way to maintain a proper professional distance is to start out on the right foot and resolve not to deviate.

This is easier to do if you come into an organization from the outside, because you start with a relatively clean slate. The politics of friendship is not an issue.

A harder situation is if you come up within the ranks of your organization to become the leader. Now you've got friends who are also your subordinates. They naturally assume that your mutual bonds of friendship and camaraderie will not change. This is a tough position for any leader to be in.

This tougher job is typical of what most head football coaches experience. Some coaches get promoted to the head coaching job at the same school where they've just been an assistant coach. Now they have authority over the same guys with whom they were recently just comrades-in-arms. This happened to me when I became the head coach at West Virginia University in 1970.

Sometimes an offensive coordinator is hired away by another school to become the new head coach. The coordinator most often takes some of his fellow assistant coaches with him to the new job.

But he and his fellow coaches have very different roles at their new school, and things cannot be the way they once were.

Either situation is difficult.

At West Virginia, when I replaced Jim Carlen as the head coach, I called my staff together and said something to this effect:

Men, I'm not a lot different from the guy I'm replacing. I have strong moral and religious convictions that carry over into work. So my expectations won't be much different from his. But for your benefit, let me go ahead and state what I believe, and what I'll be expecting from all of us. . . .

I don't remember all that I said, but I tried to make it clear that our jobs must get done consistent with my deepest convictions about our program. My biggest challenge in this regard was to be true to my word. If I said that things must be done such-and-such a way, then I had to back up my words with actions. I had to run the organization as if those beliefs really were important to me.

I never had to tell any of these coaches that my role had changed or that the nature of our relationship had changed. They knew it just like I did. My job was to ensure that I stayed true to my role by practicing what I preached.

✹

Maintaining a professional distance doesn't mean that you have to be dictatorial in your leadership style. Be yourself. Lead through your own personality. Don't try to imitate someone else. Just remember to act professionally and do what is right. The rest will take care of itself.

✳

Occasionally you'll have an employee who wants to serve the role of hall monitor. Whenever someone does something that he thinks you won't like, he'll come and tell you about it. Odds are he comes to you because he wants a closer relationship with you – perhaps because he respects you – and this is the only way he knows how to address someone of your stature.

This hasn't ever happened to me, but I've heard reports about it, and I see where it can be a problem.

If one of my coaches did that with me, I'd send him back through the proper channels. *Look,* I'd say, *you should be talking to the offensive coordinator rather than me. That's the reporting chain we follow. If the coordinator thinks it's something I should know about, he'll tell me. Otherwise, he's the person who should deal with it.* I'd be that brief, and I'd handle it that simply. We wouldn't have any further conversation about what it was he told me. And he would get the message without my having to be rude. He'll think twice before trying again to be the office tattletale.

✳

The people in your organization need good leadership more than they need good friendship from you.

✳

Good leaders in any major enterprise learn rather quickly that solitude must be embraced as a matter of course. Most of the CEOs I've ever spent time with demonstrate two qualities that impress me: they are humble people, and they act in a professional manner.

＊

A leader can be courteous, thoughtful, compassionate, and jocular with his employees without sacrificing the professional distance he must maintain.

＊

I like for my staff members to have functions without me in attendance. Such functions allow them to talk freely without worrying that I might misunderstand or misinterpret. I know they talk about things that they otherwise wouldn't discuss in my presence. Not bad things, just matters that peers tend to discuss among themselves. So I'm encouraged when there are functions where my coaches are alone together, or when they're in the limelight apart from me.

＊

A good leader has no interest in being feared. If you insist that people fear you because of the power you have, you are a sorry leader.

But a good leader leaves enough space between himself and others that he can hold them accountable. Sometimes you must be the bad guy. You are the only person authorized to assume this role.

＊

As the leader, you don't have the freedom that your subordinates have. They may not like something you do, and they may talk about it among themselves: *I don't like the way he does this . . . I don't like the way he does that.*

When I coached at Howard College back in the early 1960s, our athletic director was tight with a dollar. He didn't even allow us coaches to keep stamps in our offices. If we wanted to mail a letter, we had to see him. He kept all the stamps in his desk drawer. Now, we coaches talked about how dumb that was. We said stuff among ourselves that we would never say to him. So I understand that my staff members may make similar judgments about me.

But as the head coach, I am not allowed to do the same thing. I will not pull one of my staff members aside and say, *Man, Coach Smith is acting like a baby.*

The reasons why I cannot do this should be obvious.

✳

People will treat you like a leader as long as you act like one. They expect more out of you than they do of their peers.

19
ENTHUSIASM

← ———————————————————→

Enthusiasm makes a player jump higher,
hit harder, and run faster.

The word *enthusiasm* means, literally, to be filled with divine spirit. *Enthusiasm* comes from the Greek words *en* (meaning "in") and *theos* (meaning "god"). Enthusiastic people possess a dynamism and an inner drive that seems divinely inspired. They go beyond our average expectations because they are *en-thused . . . filled with the power of divinity*.

David, a 40-point underdog to Goliath, was enthused. Moses was enthused. Deborah was enthused. Samson was enthused. The prophets were enthused. And Jesus was enthused.

That ain't bad company, no matter what business you're in.

✳

Enthusiasm can accomplish what every other effort has failed to do.

One of my most dramatic reminders of this occurred on November 26, 1994.

It was the last game of the regular season and the Florida Gators were in town. This annual match-up is the biggest game of the regular season for both teams. Coaching careers have been made and broken over this rivalry.

These games are always a toss-up because the rivalry is so intense. Some years Florida will be favored and we will give them fits on their own home field. And sometimes it works just the opposite. But one thing you know for sure: the kids will practice hard all week for this game. A river of adrenaline floods the stadium when each team races onto the turf. And players from both teams will leave their best efforts on the field of battle. Enthusiasm isn't a problem for either side when this game rolls around.

Of course, we had the home-field advantage in '94 (and I thought the better team), so I figured our kids would find a way to pull this one out.

Florida's players, however, thought differently.

Those guys from Gainesville manhandled us for three quarters. I mean, if you were a Florida State fan, it was both ugly and demoralizing. Nothing we tried to do was working. Every drive fizzled. Our punter's leg was getting sore from too many fourth downs. Meanwhile, Florida's young quarterback, Danny Wuerffel, was picking us apart with his short, crisp passes. He was playing like some kind of Heisman Trophy candidate. And the Florida defense refused to let us into the endzone.

They led 24-3 at halftime, and 31-3 with just over 10 minutes left in the fourth quarter.

I paced the sidelines like a man possessed. Our fans thought I was brainstorming for a miracle. Actually, I was practicing my concession speech. Steve Spurrier and his staff had done an excellent job preparing for us.

When our fullback pounded up the middle for our first touchdown with just over 10 minutes remaining, I felt a little relieved. At least we now had 10 points. 31-10 ain't nearly as bad as 31-3, because our potent offense at least got one touchdown. That's about as much optimism as I could muster.

But something was happening among my players that I didn't recognize at the time. They were getting fired up all over again. After getting their noses bloodied for three straight quarters by some fine athletes on the other side of the ball, they suddenly remembered that they weren't bad athletes themselves.

We kicked off trailing 31-10 and our defense forced Florida to punt. Danny Kanell, our quarterback, led us on a three-play touchdown drive covering 72 yards. It's now 31-17 with 10:04 left in the game. My loser's speech began to look a little more respectable.

We kicked off and held them again. Now I began to wonder, *Could we? Is it possible? Nah. Not enough time. If our offense gets stopped even once, we're done for.* Heck, after getting mashed for three quarters, I wouldn't let myself get too optimistic.

My players, however, weren't nearly as sophisticated in their thinking. They actually thought we could win. What's more, they smelled blood in the water.

Florida punted the ball inside our own 30-yard line. Several swing passes to running back Warrick Dunn got us close to their goal line. Danny Kanell went in on a quarterback keeper, and suddenly the score was 31-24 with 5:25 left. The players and fans were ecstatic. I'd never seen the crowd so wild with excitement. As for me, I was having one of those dadgum betwixt-and-between moments. My head told me, *No way we can win*, while my heart kept saying, *Dare to believe!*

Sure enough, on Florida's next drive, the wide receiver cut inside when Wuerffel expected him to cut outside. Our cornerback made a diving interception on our own 39-yard line. Only minutes remained. On the very next play, Warrick Dunn caught a swing pass in the flat and ran all the way down to Florida's 23. Several plays later, we ran it in from the five with 1:45 left in the game.

31-31!

Unbelievable! Who'd have ever thought it possible? I know two guys that night who didn't: Steve Spurrier and me.

But that's not all. Our defense held Florida one more time and we got the ball back with only seconds to go. We tried to quickly pass the ball within field-goal range, but the clock ran out and the game ended.

As we ran off the field, a TV sportscaster stuck a microphone in my face and asked what I thought about the game. *It was one of the greatest wins . . . I mean COMEBACKS. . . in Florida State history*, I blurted out.

It sure felt like a win.

And it was all due to enthusiasm.

＊

Football, like any other activity in life, is at least 50 percent emotion. Find an accountant or doctor who is totally disinterested in his job and, no matter how intelligent and skillful he is, he'll probably make mistakes due to complacency. I'll bet most automobile accidents occur because at least one driver isn't paying attention. Complacency is a pervasive phenomenon and a real threat to success.

People perform best when they are excited about their work.

＊

Nothing scares me on game day like the absence of enthusiasm.

＊

Here are four great truths I've learned about enthusiasm over the past 50 years:

1. People are not always going to be enthusiastic.

Enthusiasm rises and falls like the tides. We simply cannot get our players excited about every game. They aren't dummies. They know the difference between Miami and Western Carolina. It's my job to keep the players as enthusiastic as possible, but I don't fret when the tide goes out.

I just look to my team leaders.

Those are the guys I can expect to be enthusiastic when enthusiasm is needed. They'll lead the others in the right direction.

2. When enthusiasm is likely to be low, you must become more vigilant not to allow complacency and carelessness.

On weeks when a lack of enthusiasm is likely to be a problem, I stress with my coaches the absolute importance of not letting up. *Pay attention to details,* I remind them. *Watch the players closely in practice to make sure that they're doing what we've asked of them, and get on them if they're slacking.* Discipline and attention to detail help to ensure that a letdown does not get us beat on Saturday.

3. Meet regularly with the people in the trenches to remind them how valuable that day's work is to the success of the program.

Come August, I want my best eleven players on each side of the ball for the first day of practice. To know who belongs on the first team, I need their best during spring practice. So I meet with them in hopes of encouraging their best efforts. I follow the same routine during the regular season. Every day on the practice field is valuable. I don't want to waste a single occasion to get better.

Knowledge is power. I want my players empowered. If they aren't enthused enough to work hard during practice, how can my coaches gauge their true strengths and weaknesses as a team?

4. At crunch time, when productivity must be at its highest, look for ways to get people fired up.

Our crunch time occurs on the weekend, and I talk with my players on three occasions during that time. First, I have them all together on Friday night before the game. Second, I have them all together in the locker room just before the game. And third, I have them together at halftime.

Here are some things I do to maintain the level of enthusiasm I believe is needed at any given moment:

✗ I appeal to their competitive spirit.

These are well-conditioned athletes who aren't afraid of a challenge on the field. They've tasted victory before and enjoyed it. *Are you gonna let these other guys come in here and beat you?* I might ask. *Are you gonna let them push you around and whip your tails?*

✗ I appeal to their pride.

Our players made names for themselves in high school. They once were special, and now they can be special again. Plus, we've worked them hard enough in practices and during our winter conditioning drills that they all should feel some pride of accomplishment. So I appeal to their personal pride. *You've done all that we've asked of you,* I might say. *You are ready, and you're more than able. Now all these faces will be watching you today, to see how tough you are, how dedicated you are. What are you going to show them? What are you gonna let them think about you?*

✗ I appeal to past accomplishments by citing the great teams that have played in prior years, teams that upheld our high standards of success and refused to let the streak of great seasons end.

✗ I use negative reinforcement when appropriate.

Negative reinforcement occurs in the form of *bulletin-board material.* If a player or coach makes an unguarded statement in the media that reflects poorly on the other team, coaches sometimes post these comments on the locker-room bulletin board for players to read. The purpose, of course, is to get players fired up over what the opponent has said. I'll oftentimes read such comments to my players and then challenge them to offer their response on the field.

I usually save this information for Friday night before the game. If I tell the players earlier in the week, they may beat up on one another so much in practice that no one's healthy for Saturday's game. Timing is the key with bulletin-board motivation.

✳

I like for my players to show enthusiasm on the field. I realize that the rules don't allow for taunting. I agree with the rules. A player who makes a great play should act like he's been there before and never try to publicly humiliate his opponent beyond outplaying him.

At the same time, I hate to see kids penalized for getting excited after scoring a touchdown or creating a turnover. These guys have practiced hard all year. They live for these eleven games.

When I was a college player, we usually didn't show much emotion after scoring a touchdown. That's just the way it was back in those days. You crossed the goal line and acted as if it was all in a day's work. If everyone did things according to my preferences, players would still act this way today.

But times are different now. Kids get excited. What a shame to penalize them for acting excited, jumping up and down, or otherwise celebrating with their teammates after making a great play.

＊

Sometimes the best way to motivate your employees is to get one of them excited, and let that person motivate the others.

Corey Simon, now playing for the Philadelphia Eagles, was one of my best motivators on our 1999 national championship team. He could really arouse enthusiasm among his teammates. I think part of his motivational success lay in the fact that he could physically handle just about anyone on the team, and they knew it. So when he said, *Let's work hard,* they worked hard.

It helps to have one or two folks in the trenches who are both excitable and respected by their peers.

＊

I will reveal the biggest reason we lost the 2000 Orange Bowl game to Oklahoma for the national championship: ENTHUSIASM – or in our case, the lack of it.

Oklahoma's players and staff were much more excited than us to play in the national championship game. It was obvious to anyone who watched. Our players thought they had an easy opponent, while Oklahoma's players were hungry and fired up. They outplayed us the entire game.

They beat us in enthusiasm, and they beat us for the national championship.

Their coaches did a great job.

20
RELATING TO
SUPERIORS

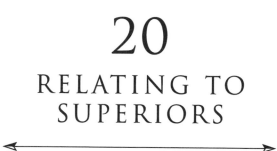

I owe to those above what I expect from those below.

If your job doesn't require you to answer to anyone, skip this chapter.

I'm not in that position.

Being the leader of a football program does not mean I have *carte blanche* authority to do as I please. Effective leadership requires me to be a follower as well as a leader. I answer directly to the athletic director at my institution. The athletic director answers to the president. And the president answers to our board of regents. All of us are accountable to someone.

✳

In regard to day-to-day operations, my superiors and I communicate on a "need to know" basis.

My superiors tell me what I need to know – such as what my budget will be for the coming year, what new school policies relate directly to my program, and so forth. We enjoy a good relationship because they don't involve me in issues or decisions that lie beyond my level of authority. That's as it should be. I use the same operating procedure when dealing with them.

There's a fine line, of course, between telling them too much and telling them too little about what's going on in my program. If I tell them too much, I invite unnecessary meddling. If I tell them too little, I open myself up to censure, discipline, and perhaps restrictions on my authority.

Common sense, along with a familiarity with institutional or company policy, is the best guide in these matters. If a player is accused of a crime, that's obviously something my A.D. needs to know because we have school policies for dealing with such issues. If the player has been missing too many classes, my coaches will discipline the athlete internally and no one will be the wiser.

As a working rule, remember that fewer policies are better than more policies. The minute you start laundering your problems in public, your superiors will feel obligated to create a new rule or procedure to fix the problem. The more problems you take to them, the more rules you'll be saddled with. My advice is to handle matters internally and confidentially whenever possible.

Use Occam's Razor as your guide: Never multiply entities (in this case, rules) beyond necessity.

✳

Because I hold a high-profile job, the media sometimes reports on issues over which I might disagree with the school's athletic director or president. And though a reporter might not aim to stir up controversy, he most likely will report any he discovers. One of my jobs is to ensure that no such public controversy arises.

Toward this end, and especially when talking with the media, I try to follow several rules in regard to my superiors. These rules work well in any leadership venue:

- ✗ Do not paint your superiors into a corner by using ill-advised language.
- ✗ Do not issue an ultimatum.
- ✗ Leave both yourself and your superiors an "out" so that no one is made to look bad, regardless of the final decision that is made.
- ✗ Do not try to force their hand by any other means.

Most high-level executives I've known are fairly smart people. They've been around the block a few times and deal frequently with complicated issues. University presidents fall into that category. I've never had a president who used the media or any other public venue to force my hand on an issue. Even if we sharply disagreed in private, the presidents I've worked for have always been respectful and protective of me in public.

I've learned the wisdom of that approach. The fiercest lion is a cornered lion. It has no choice but to fight. I've watched a number of professional athletes blast their coach or franchise owner in public over some internal disagreement. Then the media jumps all over it, and the coach or owner is forced to solve the problem in the press. Everyone is made to look bad. And the player's superiors now have strong emotional reasons to oppose the player's wishes.

When I told my athletic director in January 2001 that I planned to name my son Jeff as the new offensive coordinator, he took this information to the university president. The president, of course, was the one person who would take the heat if a charge of nepotism arose. He had to be cautious, and he implied in a newspaper interview that Jeff's chance of getting the appointment was slim. It's what he didn't say, however, that revealed his good judgment. He never said Jeff's appointment was IMPOSSIBLE.

In retrospect, you can see the wisdom of his ways. After all, he had made decisions in other nepotism cases of which I was unaware, and he had to be consistent in his enforcement of the school's anti-nepotism policy. I met with him in private to explain why I thought appointing Jeff as coordinator was different from a department head who appointed his son to a tenure-track position. He listened to my argument but didn't appear persuaded. Nonetheless, I never forced him to make a decision on the spot, and he didn't offer one.

The whole situation left me on edge. I walked out of that meeting with no feel for the decision he would make. When the media interviewed him on the subject of hiring Jeff as coordinator, I had a strong feeling that Jeff wouldn't get the job.

To make a long story short, the issue was more serious than I allowed to be known. Jeff's appointment wasn't the real issue from my vantage point. The real issue was the future success of my football program. We had lost 14 starters from the previous year, our former offensive coordinator left to take another job, and we had just lost the national championship game to Oklahoma. Continuity in our program was of paramount importance. Selecting the right offensive coordinator was critical. I was frustrated enough over this nepotism issue to consider retiring if my decision was overruled. From my side of the field, I felt that no one knew better than me who would fit best in that coordinator's role. Yet I understood the president's dilemma and his responsibility to an entire university.

Thankfully, the president never came out publicly and said, *We can't do it*. He never said, *I won't allow it*. Such an act would have then forced my hand on the early retirement issue. What he did was to send the matter through established institutional channels and receive a committee recommendation. The committee recommended Jeff's appointment to the coordinator's position, a proper reporting structure was put in place, and Jeff received the promotion.

Now if I had tried to force the president's hand in the press, or issued an ultimatum in private, I probably would've prematurely forced him to deny my request. Even when things looked bleak, I kept quiet and left the decision process in his hands. Neither of us painted the other into a corner. And in the end, it worked out well for both of us.

✻

I'd make a much better military strategist than a diplomatic negotiator. Give me my marching orders and let me work out a strategy to beat the other guy. Don't put me at the negotiating table and make me haggle with my adversary.

Why not the diplomat's role?

Because my temperament isn't suited for it. In a diplomatic dispute, I'd probably take the gloves off much too soon and simply order an attack.

I've got some colleagues in coaching who are better suited for boardroom negotiations than for tactical field planning. They are good leaders in their own right, but their skills are different from mine. They know how to build consensus, establish coalitions, and maneuver through the politics of competing wills.

That's just not my nature. I'll give you an honest word, a fair shake, and an even chance. But if you challenge my integrity after that, well, them's fightin' words.

There's an old Irish saying: *Is this a private fight, or can anyone join in?* I lived by that code as an immature teenager. My philosophy was: Be a godly young man, but don't back down from a fight if some guy tries to bully you. I had a bad habit of ending diplomatic negotiations prematurely.

When I donned the shirt and tie of adulthood, my fighting days ended. But my instincts didn't change. And since diplomacy and political maneuvering didn't come naturally, I adapted by learning to bite my lip.

I don't always agree with decisions made by my superiors. Sometimes I have better solutions than them because I understand football and the people who play it. Nonetheless, when we disagree, it's usually better for me to quietly accept their decisions rather than protest loudly and insist upon having my way.

＊

No one has ever held a gun to my head and forced me to work at Florida State. Or at any other job I held.

If I'm willing to accept a paycheck from the university, then I must respect decisions made by my superiors and be supportive of my institution. Carping, moaning, sniping, and back-biting are unacceptable forms of behavior. If I don't like the way things are done, I can quit my job. If I don't quit, then I have no right to publicly criticize those above me. It's that simple.

I may disagree with a decision made by my superiors. I may in fact think that a decision is absolutely wrong. But I have no right to get with my coaches, or with selected alumni, or with news reporters, and begin complaining. I expect better from my coaches in regard to me. My superiors should expect the same from me.

I'm not naïve in this regard. When we are winning games, I enjoy a certain degree of leverage that comes with success. If the athletic director or president went against my wishes, I suppose I could turn up the heat on them, maybe even create some controversy. As Bear Bryant reportedly said on one occasion, 50,000 people will show up to watch a football game, but they won't show up to watch a math test. Success provides a limited opportunity to manipulate public sentiment.

Several things hold me back from such temptations, however, and incline me to act differently.

First and foremost, I was raised to respect authority and obey those who are above me. I still believe it's the best course of action for anyone. Martin Luther King Jr. taught this lesson to Americans better than anyone. Back during the 1950s and '60s, he knew full well that segregation laws were immoral. And when he chose to defy those laws, he accepted the punishment that the law mandated. In other words, he brought about change without putting himself above the law. He could've incited riots and taken up arms, but he didn't. And look what a powerful difference he made in our society. He did it the right way by operating within the system to change the system.

Second, if I preach the concept of TEAM to my players and staff, I'm a hypocrite if I act otherwise on my own behalf. It has been my winning formula for almost 50 years. But TEAM extends above me as well as below me. I expect my players to trust my judgment when it comes to running our program. My superiors have a right to expect the same measure of trust from me. I don't always agree with what they do. Sometimes I get mad. But after telling them in private how I feel, I keep the disagreement to myself.

Heck, I need those guys.

Back at West Virginia in 1974, many of the fans wanted me fired after a 4-7 season. But the A.D. was behind me, and the president gave me his vote of confidence. With those two guys on my side, we coaches could stay focused on business. None of us bailed out and took other jobs. No one came to work depressed over job security. We had two men on our side who, whether they realized it or not, contributed significantly to our 8-3 season the following year.

✳

People who bad-mouth their superiors behind their backs are cowards. And they lack good judgment.

Anyone who has pride in himself will never say behind someone's back what he has not first said to that person's face. Or, to put it conversely, what won't be said to a person's face shouldn't be said behind his back.

If I choose to back-bite, it merely reveals that someone was able to get the best of me. They got under my skin. They won.

I won't let that happen.

*

I don't try to get chummy with my superiors, even if they are powerful trustees who think I'm the greatest thing since Santa Claus.

The easiest way for me to maintain good relations is to stay focused on my job and not worry about what my superiors think. If I'm doing my job, and they are doing their jobs, it'll all work out fine.

Anyway, the closer I draw them to me, the greater their chances of meddling in my affairs.

Some coaches try to get political and work around the system by maintaining close relations with certain powerful individuals. This maneuver might produce short-term results, but the risk usually isn't worth the reward.

The leader who plays politics in order to work outside the system had better choose his friends wisely, because he will make enemies in the process. One day those enemies may be the powerful individuals he wishes were on his side.

*

The most common problem I've observed over the years relates not to coaches but to superiors who involve themselves in matters best left to the coach or others.

This past year, an athletic director of a major university told news reporters that the head coach would be given one more year to improve his team's flagging performance. Several days later, and without consulting the A.D., the president of the school summarily fired the coach. I don't know the particulars, but it's a tough situation for both a coach and an athletic director to work under.

At another southern school, according to news reports, a former university president went on record as saying that coaches and selected trustees at his institution regularly bypassed him in the management of the school's athletics programs. That type of situation would make me very nervous as a coach.

Any coach, or any prudent leader, should do his homework before taking a job. If an organization has a history of outside interference, or of hiring and firing the lead man on a regular basis, be leery. Things probably won't change just because you show up. Even if the organization has new leadership at the top, it's no guarantee that the past won't repeat itself.

If possible, look back at what's happened over the past 10 or 15 years. The pattern you find is what you should expect if you take the job.

21
DEALING WITH
THE PUBLIC

←——————————————→

The public is fickle.

✳

When I'm winning, the fans call me *Sweet Ol' Bobby*. When I lose, they just abbreviate the name.

✳

When I address the subject of public opinion, I'm not speaking about one's need to be aware of the public's likes and dislikes. Successful businesspeople know they must always keep a finger on the pulse of public sentiment.

But public opinion should never become the barometer of our moral decision-making or our commitment to truth. *Right* and *truth* often cut against the grain of public sentiment. The world wasn't flat in the year A.D. 1400, no matter how many people believed it was. Just because people have an opinion doesn't mean their opinion is any good.

Public opinion can be intimidating. It's scary to stand out on your own. It's much more comforting to blend in with the masses . . . to talk and look and act just like everyone else . . . and to know that vast numbers of people are pleased that you see eye-to-eye with them. Modern-day emphasis on political correctness, though intended as a corrective to public opinion, is in reality just another form of mass-mindedness.

Good leaders learn to live without the transitory comforts of public approval or political correctness. You'll never please all the people all the time. So your best bet is to live by high principles, follow your own best judgment, stick to your guns in times of adversity, and let the chips fall where they may. This isn't a profound insight. But it bears repeating only because the power of public opinion can be overwhelming at times.

In regard to public opinion, *wisdom* and *courage* are the operative virtues of good leadership. Wisdom is devoted to truth and goodness. Courage is the power that makes true devotion possible.

✳

No one in Tallahassee really knew me during my first year at FSU in 1976, and I wanted to show them how good a coach I was.

Our first three games that year were on the road, and we lost all three. Our fourth game, however, was in front of my home crowd. I was excited. This game would be played in front of my own fans . . . my own friends . . . and all those alumni who cheered and slapped me on the back when I first got hired. No more playing amidst a sea of red, which was how it seemed in Oklahoma's stadium the week before. And no more loud roars from 60,000 fans cheering our every mistake. I was going to be in front of *my* people during the fourth game.

The opponent was Kansas State. We proved an even match for them. At halftime, the score was tied at 0-0. Definitely a moral victory for our young team.

Kansas State opened the second half by kicking off. We took the ball and made several first downs. Then it happened. Fourth-and-three at our own 40-yard line. My coaching experience told me to punt. Though no one had yet scored in the game, this was no time to gamble. So I sent the punt team onto the field.

BOOOOO, went the crowd. They had grown restless and eager for points. *BOOOOO* was the judgment I heard from all my supportive fans and friends and alumni.

My heart quickened as I thought to myself, *All my buddies up there in the stands want me to go for the first down, no matter what. My buddies want me to gamble. They don't want us to punt the ball away. Neither do I.*

So I hurriedly called a time-out and motioned the punt team off the field.

YEAAAAAAH, roared all my buddies in the stands. *YOU GET 'EM, COACH BOWDEN. SHOW 'EM WE'RE NOT AFRAID.*

My blood was really pumping at this point. I hurriedly called the offense together on the sideline and asked, *Do you hear the crowd behind you? They want us to go for it. What do you think? Can you do it?*

The offense nodded their agreement with the crowd, so I sent them back onto the field. We called "34 Wham," where the tail-back runs off-tackle behind the fullback.

I watched intently as the quarterback took his position behind the center.

On the snap of the ball, our offensive line surged forward. The fullback drove straight ahead off-tackle and smashed into the linebacker. The halfback followed behind him, took the hand-off from the quarterback, and bulled his way across the line of scrimmage. Players rammed into other players. Then, seconds later, the play was over. Whistles blew. Game officials waded in and began unpiling the players. One official found the ball and held it up in his hand, while another used his foot to mark the spot where the ball should be spotted. It was going to be close. My buddies in the crowd fell silent. Then the ball was set down on the turf close to the first down marker, and the chain gang was brought in for a measurement.

Finally, the referee made the call.

We fell short by a yard.

Kansas State got the ball on our 40-yard line.

And as our offense trotted off the field, my fans expressed themselves one more time: *BOOOOOOOO . . . BOOOOOOOO . . . WHY'D YOU CALL THAT PLAY, BOWDEN?*

It got real lonely down there on that sideline.

But I thought you wanted me to go for it. . . . ? ? ?

As long as I win, people will be for me. If I lose, they will want to replace me.

That's just the way it is.

And that's why I never listen to public opinion.

✳

Some people are too idealistic. To listen to their judgments, I should crucify any player who makes a serious mistake. If I don't perform the crucifixion, then I'm no better than a criminal myself. I ignore these people.

Others are naturally partisan. Our school is the enemy of their school, so everything I do is wrong. These folks don't even register on the scale.

Still others seem to have way too much free time. They fill their time looking for errors. I compare them to the people who write op-ed notes to the editor correcting a journalist's grammar. Surely they've got better things to do!

These folks notwithstanding, I do receive a lot of praise from fans. I wish it was because they all loved me, but it's not that way. Many of them simply love the sweet savour of victory. They enjoy the cathartic euphoria of conquest. And as long as my team is the conqueror, my players and I are objects of deep affection. But make no mistake. If I start losing, the cheers will turn to jeers. The halo over my head will be lowered down around my neck.

*

I will listen to public opinion, but I will not allow public senti-ment to govern my decisions. Maybe I'm stubborn in my think-ing, but too often the public wants a hanging and I don't. And too often, the most vocal segment of the public is misinformed because their insights are derived from local sports-talk radio. They are informed by the uninformed.

If I listened to public opinion, one or more of the following things would occur the week after a big loss:

✘ We would entirely revamp our offensive and/or defensive scheme in the middle of the season.

✘ We would kick some players off the team, sideline many others, and yell and scream at the rest.

✘ I would fire some of my staff.

✘ I would hang myself just after resigning in disgrace.

Ninety-nine percent of the fans don't know enough about football to offer helpful advice.

Fans do not know which players should be playing on Saturday. They only get to watch our kids on game day. We coaches see the players every day in practice. We know who is performing the best day in and day out. This is especially true at the quarterback posi-tion. Woe unto you if you have two quarterbacks of equal ability and age, one of whom is Hispanic and the other a white Anglo-Saxon. Now you'll definitely have problems with segments of the general public. If you want to get fired, listen to them.

The fans do not watch game film to determine the best schemes for attacking an opponent. We coaches have watched film on an upcoming opponent for hundreds of hours. We've studied their tendencies, evaluated their strengths and weaknesses, and know where our best chance for success lies. Even if we fail, we've played the odds to our advantage.

The fans have no idea about the personal issues that many of our players wrestle with outside of football – issues that sometimes affect their play on Saturday. A player's mother dies of cancer, another player has been practicing despite a partial shoulder separation, while another is homesick and depressed. The fans don't usually know about those kinds of problems.

I get letters all the time from fans. Some are well-intentioned. Others are convinced that I'm brain dead. They'll offer plays for me to run. They'll evaluate talent and suggest a starting line-up. They'll offer a stinging critique on some recent game – you know, the game we won by only three points but could have won by 35 if only we knew as much about football as the writer himself. I wonder how much money that guy lost on the over/under!

A leader who has done his homework is well advised to stick with his own best judgments.

* * *

One of the biggest complaints I hear is that our players are thieves and thugs. It's funny. These critics wouldn't dare make such heartless comments about their own children, but they will denounce football players in a heartbeat.

We've had a number of NFL first-round draft choices come out of

FSU over the past 15 years, all of whom have made me proud. Peter Boulware of the Baltimore Ravens is a bright young man whose father is a surgeon. Andre Wadsworth, taken by the St. Louis Cardinals, was a walk-on at FSU and a fine Christian. Corey Simon's moral character can be matched with any teammate among the Philadelphia Eagles. And Cincinnati's Peter Warrick, who is widely known for his bad decision at Dillard's department store, returned for his senior year despite being a likely first-rounder and an immediate millionaire after his junior year. In 2000, he used his own money to sponsor a camp for underprivileged children in Sarasota, Florida. Even "Neon" Deion Sanders, who is often remembered for his flamboyant style, was one of the hardest-working players we've ever had at Florida State. He never missed practice. He played when he was injured. And he played when he was in pain. Most people don't know that about him.

Other guys who starred for us also have done well. Darryl Bush, a three-year starter at linebacker, maintained a 4.0 GPA throughout college. Ken Alexander and Dave Roberts went on to law school.

We hear a lot about the few who get into trouble. This is probably the first you've heard of Corey Simon's strong moral character.

✳

I have rules, and I stick with them. But they're *my* rules, and I won't let the media or the general public dictate how I discipline my players.

In 1995, Lou Holtz called me from Notre Dame. He had recruited a gifted receiver out of West Virginia named Randy Moss. This guy was special. He had remarkable quickness, fingers like glue, and speed enough to break the sound barrier.

Now, Randy had gotten into trouble during his senior year in high school. Some student made racist remarks in class one day about Randy's friend, and Randy beat up the student. As a result, Randy was arrested and placed on parole.

Lou Holtz was subsequently told that Randy would be denied admission to Notre Dame. So Lou called and told me about the situation, suggesting that I might want him at Florida State. I did want him, and I was able to get him admitted.

When Randy came to FSU, the first thing I did was meet with him in my office. I said, *Now, Randy, you're here with two strikes against you. You can't afford to have any more problems. If you do, I'll have to let you go.*

I also told him he must redshirt one year before playing. Our school president made this request as a condition of Randy's admission to FSU. It was not an NCAA requirement.

This news of a redshirt year nearly killed Randy. He never had to sit out a single game before, much less an entire season. Plus, he was arguably the finest receiver in all of college football – though only a freshman! He knew it and we knew it. But to his credit, he accepted the conditions without complaint. He sat out that first year, his talents just wasting on the sidelines, and never once grumbled. To his further credit, he never was a problem child while at FSU. He was a model citizen.

After that redshirt season, Randy went back home to West Virginia and, well, wouldn't you know it, I open the newspaper one summer morning and read that Randy Moss had violated a condition of his parole while at home in West Virginia. Apparently he tested positive for marijuana use. What would have gone unnoticed by the media if he had been a scholarship English major was headline news because he was a scholarship football player. Be that as it may, Randy had failed to keep the terms of our agreement.

That morning at the office, I placed a phone call to Randy's attorney in West Virginia. *Is it true?* I asked. I fully expected to hear some story defending Randy's innocence. But Randy Moss is a stand-up guy. *Yes, it's true*, I was told. So I dismissed him from the team.

Randy really wanted to play at FSU. He offered to relinquish his scholarship and pay his own way for school, if I would keep him on the team. I couldn't do it. Rules are rules. I couldn't afford to set a precedent that I might regret down the road. So Randy left FSU and transferred to Marshall, where he became an All-American and an eventual first-round draft choice by the Minnesota Vikings.

I tell you that story because of what happened three years later with Peter Warrick. Pete did something at a local department store that he knew he shouldn't do. He allowed a store clerk to sell clothes at a drastic discount to him and another player. The other player was Laveranues Coles. Laveranues was the fastest player on our team and, along with Peter, a starting wide receiver. What Peter, Laveranues, and the store clerk did was wrong.

When the story broke, I dismissed Laveranues from the team but only suspended Peter, pending a final verdict on the case. That's the gist of the story known to the nation: Coles was out, Warrick was still in. And here's what I heard in response: *Three years ago you dismissed Randy Moss from your team. And now you've kicked Coles off the team. But Peter Warrick, your current Heisman Trophy candidate, is being kept on the team for a very obvious reason: You need him to win a national championship this year.*

It sounds great, but it's a ridiculous charge. Laveranues Coles is a good young man whom I really liked. But he'd been in my doghouse on two prior occasions, and I told him that summer that if he did anything else, I'd have to let him go. Laveranues was not only the fastest player on our team, but he was also a great athlete and an NFL prospect. The New York Jets ended up drafting him in the third round in 1999. But team rules are team rules. Randy's situation fell into the same category, knowing as he did that he had two strikes against him when he first showed up in Tallahassee. Both guys knew what the consequences would be, and they accepted their dismissal without complaint. Peter Warrick, however, had not been in trouble before. People who wanted me to treat him by the same standard totally missed the fact that I WAS treating him by the same standard.

Can you imagine how good we might have been with Moss, Coles, and Warrick on the same field, all catching passes from 2000 Heisman winner Chris Weinke? I lost two of my three best receivers over a two-year period.

I have rules. I try to apply those rules evenly and fairly. And I stick with them. Public opinion will not sway me one way or another.

22
THE MEDIA

←――――――――――――――――――→

People in the media have a job to do.
They're trying to earn a living, just like me.

The news media is the most powerful force in athletics today. As most seasoned coaches know, you'd better get them on your side, and for heaven's sake don't lie or try to deceive them, because they will eat you alive.

Personally, I enjoy the media.

I treat them with the same high regard that I show to high school coaches. If high school coaches don't cooperate with us when we visit their schools, we cannot be successful. We need reliable information on their players, and we hope the coaches will not assume an adversarial posture or work to undermine our efforts. So we assist these high school coaches in whatever ways we can. We invite them to our coaching clinics. We try to get them on the sidelines during a ballgame. And I'll take the time to meet with any high school coach who wishes to talk with me. We can't win the recruiting war without their help.

I also need the media.

When I first came to FSU in 1976, we needed all the media exposure we could get. I made time for every interview opportunity that came along. The media was the only good way to get my message out to fans across the state of Florida.

✳

I've enjoyed a favorable reputation with the media since being at Florida State, and I've worked hard for that reputation.

Part of my success owes to my appreciation of the difficult job they have. Sportswriters are obligated to write a new story every day. They've got to dig up something interesting to say, without fail, day after day after day. Goodness, I couldn't write an interesting new story once a month, much less once a day!

Consequently, I try to make myself accessible and give them something interesting to write about, perhaps some insight or observation they might be interested to know.

✳

I've never resented the role of the media in sports. Some coaches do. Personally, it seems foolish to argue with people who buy ink by the barrel.

I don't expect reporters to write only things that I like. These folks have a right to disagree with me and express their true beliefs. I do, however, expect them to be fair and balanced in their reporting. If a writer lies or takes backhanded shots at me in the media, then I won't talk to that guy anymore. I'll just tell my secretary, *Next time*

*he calls for an interview, tell him I'm mad at him, and that I'm not
available for any more interviews with him at the present time.*

The only sportswriter I ever had a real problem with was from
Wheeling, West Virginia, back when I coached at WVU in the early
'70s. This fellow seemed to have a genuine dislike for me. After one
particularly heartbreaking homecoming loss to our arch rival
Pittsburgh, he started referring to me in print as "Bobby
Bowdown." His articles got very personal. He wrote that I was a
lousy coach who knew little about football and who wouldn't last
long as a head coach. The tone of his columns was clearly vindictive.

I eventually told my sports information director not to give this
guy a pressbox pass to any more of our ballgames. The guy could
get his story from the radio play-by-play for all I cared. I certainly wasn't going to help his career by opening the door to my football program. Fair is fair, and he wasn't playing fairly at all.

The only other comparable situation occurred in 1994, just
months after we won the 1993 national championship. A writer
for *Sports Illustrated* showed up in my office one day for an interview. Shortly before his arrival, our athletic director had called me
to say, *Watch out, Bobby. Something's up.*

What the writer knew, and I didn't know, was that the infamous
Foot Locker episode had just occurred, in which a sports agent had
taken several of our players to a retail store and bought $6,000
worth of tennis shoes and other clothing items for them.

If you aren't in coaching, you need to understand that the coach
is often the last person to know about such episodes. The media
will sometimes get wind of a rumor and then call to ask me
about it. Sometimes they'll drop by the police department and

check the arrest record for the past month, then call me for a comment. Players, of course, aren't likely to come and tell me they were arrested for disorderly conduct, and they certainly won't tell me if they've accepted new shoes from a willing buyer. Reporters are sometimes the first people to make me aware of these situations.

Such was the case with this writer from *Sports Illustrated*, and I told him that I was hearing about it for the first time from him. Well, to make a long story short, he sat right there in my office and essentially accused me of being a liar. I knew that our players had done this, he insisted, and I was "covering up" to protect myself and my winning program. His investigation would expose me for the liar I really was.

Knowing he was wrong only made me angrier.

When he left my office, I vowed never to grant him another interview.

Some guys decide to make the facts fit the theory rather than making the theory fit the facts. This guy was suffering from a severe case of invincible ignorance. No fact would be allowed to change his theory. Fortunately, guys like him are exceptions to the rule.

✳

I believe that most members of the media can be trusted to do the right thing.

In 1975, after WVU's Peach Bowl win over Lou Holtz's North Carolina State squad, I was sitting alone in the coaches' locker room. All the other coaches had dressed and gone. A single reporter lingered with me. He and I had developed a good friendship over the years and, when he asked about my future, I let it slip that I would be taking the job at FSU. No one except my wife and a few folks at Florida State knew about my decision. My words should have been more guarded.

The reporter was stunned by my disclosure. He turned to me and said, *Bobby, I can't sit on news like this. I have to report it.*

The thought horrified me for a moment. I wanted to do things on my timetable, not his. I didn't want him taking a private comment and making it public knowledge. But, the truth be told, he was being honest with me, and straightforward, in the privacy of that locker room. He could've said nothing to me at all, and just gone out and printed the article for next morning's paper. But instead of being underhanded, he discussed the issue with me. So I asked if he would please not report that he got the news directly from me. He promised. And he kept his promise.

He's typical of most sportswriters I've known well. They'll usually be fair to you if they perceive you're being fair with them.

✳

I won't try to mislead the media. Most of them are good at what they do. If I mislead them, they'll probably figure it out. Then I lose credibility and my problem becomes 10 times worse.

✳

If I were running a large corporation, I'd probably designate one person to be our company's media spokesperson. No sense having a number of people making contrary statements on the same issue. I wish we could have a single spokesperson for our football program, but we cannot.

In my profession, the media needs access to both coaches and players. The players can get in front of a microphone and say anything that crosses their minds. I repeatedly advise our players never to say anything detrimental about their own team or the other team. Negative statements *will* show up in print, because negative statements are newsworthy.

The way I figure it, these players might as well learn during college what it's like to be a public figure and deal with the media.

❉

Last year at Penn State, Joe Paterno taught us all a lesson about sticking to your principles despite media hostility.

Joe's starting quarterback was accused of assault and battery on a police officer. According to reports in the paper, the quarterback and another friend had beaten a white police officer who was with a black woman. The national press was all over the story. Few could resist the temptation to rush to judgment. The quarterback was obviously guilty, the stories screamed out, and should immediately be dismissed from the team.

But Paterno stood by his guy. Innocent until proven guilty. The kid would not be dismissed until the evidence proved otherwise.

Many members of the news media outside of University Park, Pennsylvania, responded with outrage. The lovable "Joe Pa," it now seemed obvious, was really no better than anyone else when it came to winning. He took his place in a long line of coaches who kept criminals on the team in order to win. The courts would have to pry this player out of Paterno's grip, because Joe lacked the moral rectitude to dismiss him. The story continued to be front-page news in sports pages and on news shows around the country.

But Paterno stood by his guy. And the more inflamed the media rhetoric became, the more firmly Joe dug in.

Fortunately for Joe, his athletic director and president were behind him. They supported him because they had known him too long to question his integrity. And in the end, the player was found innocent of all charges.

Now you tell me, how do you think the football players at Penn State feel about Joe Paterno? And how do you think the parents of young high school recruits will measure this man? He didn't bend to media criticism. He didn't take the easy way out. And he allowed his reputation to be sullied by folks who always manage to get the last word.

This time, Joe got the last word.

23
HANDLING SUCCESS

←——————————————————→

Complacency is the number-one threat to continued success.

Success and failure represent life on the boundaries. They represent *more* or *less* of something than we are accustomed to having. Consequently, both success and failure put a strain on our value systems.

Success works in a positive direction. It feeds the ego by offering new opportunities and new freedoms. You can get away with a lot of stuff if you're also very successful.

Failure works in a negative direction. It attacks the ego by denying certain opportunities and freedoms. You can drown in a sea of self-pity and resentment when facing adversity.

Both success and failure challenge not only your value system, but also your capacity for leadership. One promises that *the world is your oyster*. The other mocks that *goodness counts for nothing*.

✳

After 14 straight top-four finishes in the polls, one adversary rears its menacing head high above all others: COMPLACENCY.

Complacency is the number-one threat to continued success.

Complacency won't keep you from getting to the top. But it sure will keep you from staying there.

✳

Players on a championship team are more prone to complacency than players on a losing team. Losers get disillusioned. They lose confidence, lose heart, and then lose more games.

Champions, on the other hand, are prone to see themselves as having arrived. They've already done what it takes to get to the top. They worked hard, listened to their coaches, and did everything asked of them. Now that the championship has been attained, they don't need to pay nearly as much attention to all the little details. They don't need to practice as diligently or push themselves as hard as last year because, hey, they've arrived.

Yeah, sure.

I wish someone had told the Oklahoma Sooners last year how good we were. Our guys were going for a repeat of the national championship. We had more seniors in the starting lineup, more All-Americans on our team, and more depth from top to bottom than Oklahoma. But Oklahoma walked away with our trophy.

Why?

Because their players and coaches were hungry for victory.

Complacency can occur within the coaching staff as well. After a successful season, the coaches may start letting players get away with the little things that get you beat. *Old Smith played great last year,* a coach might be thinking, *so I won't need to push him as hard this year. He knows what he needs to do.* So Smith isn't challenged to take his game to a higher level. He isn't even asked to work as hard as he did last year.

As I've said so many times, players play the way they practice.

I remind my staff each year to guard against complacency. I harp on it at our annual hideaway meeting each July. And the message is carried over into our regular staff meetings during the year.

If we get complacent, it's my fault, because I'm the only person with sufficient authority to ensure that every coach does his job with the appropriate intensity and attention to detail.

✸

I recall the exact occasion when I learned this great lesson about complacency.

It was late December 1972. I was completing my third year as the head coach at WVU, and we were playing Lou Holtz's NC State team in the Peach Bowl in Atlanta, Georgia. My team was favored, and I was eager to play the game.

I'd never been the head coach in a bowl game on this level before, and I felt the bowl was a reward for the players. Consequently, I put few restrictions on them, other than to work hard in practice and play hard during the game. What they did on their own time was none of my business, provided they obeyed our team rules and stayed out of trouble. We practiced hard each day. We had a good game plan. And we were ready.

When kickoff came, the ceiling fell in on my team. We couldn't do anything right and lost the game 49-13. Everyone associated with the program felt miserable. Some people were downright angry.

When we got back home to Morgantown, all kinds of bad rumors were circulating. Some news reports said our players had been out drinking all night before the game. Others cited boosters who entered players' hotel rooms and found empty whiskey bottles in the trash cans.

Whether these reports were true stories or sour grapes, I don't know, but the ordeal taught me a valuable lesson: You better not get lax when you are successful. I was lax with my players. This was a bowl game. I regarded it as a reward. But I gave the players too much freedom, and they ended up acting just like college kids – they had a good time but abused their freedom.

I got strict after that. Better to be restrictive and then loosen up, than to start loose and then try to pull in the reins. I didn't want to be criticized again for being too lax in discipline. And I didn't want to lose again.

I faced a much-improved Lou Holtz team again in 1975. This time I worked hard to keep everyone focused on the task at hand. We won the bowl game. And there were no bad rumors floating around afterwards.

I took the job at Florida State a few weeks later. Since then, we've been to bowls all but three years, and my players set an NCAA record with 14 consecutive bowl games without a defeat.

The 1972 Peach Bowl taught me a very important lesson about the danger of success. Just because you've learned to drive doesn't mean you can take your hands off the wheel.

We are fortunate at Florida State to hold the records for most consecutive bowl wins and most bowl games without a loss in NCAA history. Our success is mostly due to determined athletes, hard work, and attention to detail by our staff. The hard work and attention to detail protect against complacency.

Still, I want our kids to have fun while they're at the bowl. I want football itself to be fun. So when we go to a bowl game, I tell my players, *Work hard when it's time to work. And play hard when it's time to play, provided you're having a good clean time.* I can't tell 21- and 22-year-old players much more about what to do when they're out on their own. They're grown men. But my coaches and I will continually remind them of why we've come to town. And we make sure that players attend to the little things in practice that help win ballgames.

＊

Someone once told me about an old Greek myth called *The Ring of Gyges.* It was the story of a shepherd boy (Gyges) who found a magic ring. The ring allowed him to be invisible. Unfortunately for others, he used his new power to seduce the queen and slay the king. The myth raises an interesting question for all of us, namely, *Would we live differently if we could get away with it?*

The ancient Greeks had a word – *hubris* – to describe human pride run amok. *Hubris* is nothing less than thinking ourselves greater than we really are. Stepping outside the boundaries drawn for us, we find that we've just stepped over the edge of a cliff. A falling-off point. We fall from good into an abyss of evil.

Sexual promiscuity is one of those abysses created by success.

✳

Aside from complacency or laxness, sexual promiscuity is the other great danger of success. Many a good leader has ruined his career by thinking he can eat the fruit of whatever tree pleases his eye.

And believe me, if you're a successful leader, you pass by more than one such tree.

I'll never forget the time when I was an assistant coach at Florida State back in the early 1960s. On one particular recruiting trip, I checked into my motel room, then went to visit a local booster. He was a very wealthy guy who owned several businesses and was a great supporter of our athletic program. I figured this would be a good relationship to nurture. It turned out to be one of my most awkward recruiting experiences.

While I was at his house talking with him, it became apparent that he and I played by different domestic rules. He enjoyed women excessively, and when his business associates visited town, he arranged female companionship for them. As he told me these things, I could tell he was trying to get a fix on me. I, on the other hand, had just met the guy and was trying not to appear self-righteous. Then he hit me with it: *Bobby, there's a teacher here in town who's just dying to meet you. She thinks you're a really great guy. I'd like for you to meet her.*

Well, I'm not perfect, but I knew this was something I didn't want. As best I could, I tried to beg off and let him know I wasn't interested in his plan. I no longer remember what I said to him that evening. I just remember leaving his house and hearing him tell me, *Maybe we can stop by your motel room later this evening.* Of course, *we* was him and the teacher.

I got back to my room and started praying. *Lord, please don't let them come by here.* I didn't want to have to deal with this situation. The thought of alienating one of the school's most generous benefactors was unpleasant, and the thought of the alternative was even worse. I wanted God to sort this one out for me.

Well, they never came to my motel room that night. I can only guess that he sensed my uneasiness and left well enough alone.

I've seen it happen all too often. A coach is on the road. Maybe his wife is angry over his extended absence from home, while he feels frustrated that his job requirement has become a family problem. Or maybe a guy is just unhappy in his marriage. Who knows? The scenarios are as varied as the people in them. But for one reason or another, a decision is made to step over the line, and once the step is made, it can never be undone.

The leader has just jeopardized his moral reputation.

Now add success to the formula. People not only think you're great, but they also want to treat you like a king. Your every wish is their command. They can think of nothing better than to cater to your whims. So you let it be known that Miss So-and-So is attractive, or better yet, you tell her yourself. Next thing you know, two people share a secret, and one of those people isn't you.

These secrets may remain undercover as long as you're successful. The people who know don't seem to mind all that much . . . until you start losing. Then suddenly the secret becomes a disdainful character flaw. And the character flaw is linked to your failure. The same people who once laughed at your indiscretion now pity your predicament. But they can't undo your new reputation as a cheater. And they can't resolve the problems you now have. So the secret comes back with a disastrous twist, all the more disastrous because it happens to be true.

You know of such instances, and so do I. There's no need to call names.

✳

If you can be the same person, come success or failure, then you've got your feet on solid ground. People can follow you with the confidence that they won't be misled.

✳

Failure tests a leader's character. Success shapes his reputation.

24
DEALING WITH
ADVERSITY

The finest steel must first pass through the hottest fire.

A leader's greatest challenge is adversity.

It's the ultimate test of character, composure, and faith in a cause.

※

Look at the football programs scandalized by cheating. Look at businesses ruined by illegal behavior. Look at politicians corrupted by power. You will find two common themes: (i) adversity, and (ii) loss of faith in what is good.

※

There are two things a person should do to deal with the storms of adversity.

First and most important, proper steps should be taken before the storm ever comes. Once the winds howl and huge waves pummel the ship, it's too late to batten the hatches and pull down the mainsail. A sailor's worst nightmare is to get caught unprepared in a storm. A ship that's prepared for bad weather will sail much more safely through the storm.

I view adversity, in all its forms, as a test of my faith in God. If I develop the habit of trusting God on a regular basis with the myriad little problems that constitute daily life, then I'm prepared when the larger issue of adversity arises.

As I've said before, YOU PLAY LIKE YOU PRACTICE. If you practice good technique when the game isn't on the line, you're more apt to perform well at game time. If I had to choose between good habits and high enthusiasm among my players in a big game, I'd take good habits every time. Enthusiasm ebbs and flows. Good habits are dependable.

So before the storm comes, develop a strategy for dealing with life and start practicing it.

Second, when adversity strikes, identify the most vulnerable point and direct your energies toward it. As a leader, your top priority is the welfare of your troops. If you can discern their most vulnerable points during adversity, you can intervene effectively on their behalf.

I know that my assistant coaches will feel much worse than I after a big loss. The onus is on me, as the head coach, to ensure that adversity doesn't cause us to lose sight of our priorities. Here's where our staff meeting devotionals have their greatest effect.

✳

My first taste of adversity as a major college head coach occurred in my first year at West Virginia.

We were playing Duke in our homecoming game, and the stadium was filled with students and visiting alumni. Midway through the fourth quarter, down by six, our offense faced fourth and four on Duke's 31-yard line. This is normally a field-goal opportunity, but our kicker's foot was not very reliable from that distance. So I asked my defensive coordinator, *If I go for the field goal and we miss it, can you keep Duke backed up in their own territory?* All he could tell me was that he didn't know.

I decided we should punt the ball and back Duke up inside their own 10-yard line. All we needed was a short squib kick of 20 yards, and then we'd do our best to hold Duke to four downs.

Well, the punter kicked the ball clean out of the endzone and up into the stands. Duke got the ball at the 20, made a few first downs, and we lost our best chance to win the game.

Fans booed me mercilessly for my decision. The local media trashed me on Sunday morning. For the first time in my life I was a villain to the public. It hurt. I felt ashamed, and I questioned whether or not I was a good coach.

After wrestling with this issue for several days, I made a deliberate decision to *get mentally tough or get out of coaching.*

I learned some tough lessons at the expense of those West Virginians. They are a great, proud people and I let them down that day. But I also let myself down when I allowed adversity to crawl so deeply under my skin. If I was going to succeed in coaching, I'd have to be mentally tough.

*

Adversity in football has taken various forms during my career. Here are a few occasions that really tested me as a head coach:

1. In 1972, in a game I thought we had a chance to win, my WVU team lost 62-14 to Joe Paterno's Penn State team. I sat in the locker room afterwards and felt like quitting. That beating took everything out of me. Years later, I learned that John Cappelletti, Penn State's Heisman-winning halfback, had promised his younger brother he'd score four touchdowns that game. The younger brother was dying from leukemia. Cappelletti got all four of 'em, just like he promised. Someone made a movie about it. All I knew at the time was that I felt like a failure.

2. In 1974, during a dismal 4-7 season, a few unhappy West Virginians demonstrated their disapproval of my coaching ability. One ignited an M-80 in my residential mailbox. Another phoned our home with death threats against my youngest daughter. Paint was poured on our family car. A steel brick was thrown against my front door. Disparaging banners were displayed around town, and some college students hanged me in effigy. And those were just the fans . . . the one's that liked me!

3. In 1976, my first season at FSU, we lost five of our first seven ballgames. We finished the season with a 5-6 record. I privately wondered if I was the wrong guy for the job.

4. In 1986, an FSU starting lineman named Pablo Lopez – a wonderful human being blessed with great ability – was shot and killed while trying to stop a fight at a fraternity party. I still miss that kid.

5. In 1990, just prior to our eighth ballgame against South Carolina, someone wrote a letter threatening to assassinate me during the game. According to his letter, he had lost a lot of money betting on us the week before, when we lost to Auburn 20-17. Now he was going to get even.

I kept the news a secret from my staff and family. Local law enforcement got involved, and no one noticed their added presence in the stadium during the South Carolina game.

The gunman either missed me or never tried it. We didn't let that story get out to the press until after the season. I was afraid some other nut might read about it and think it was a good idea.

6. In February 2001, a freshman linebacker named Devaughn Darling passed out and died while participating with his teammates in our winter conditioning drills. The conditioning exercises are rigorous and exhausting. But in my 50 years of conducting these drills, nothing like this had ever happened before. I tell the parents of my recruits, *I'll be watching over your son. I'll be watching out for him.* With Devaughn it was easy, because he came from such an outstanding family. But I couldn't help him on this occasion. Our trainers and doctors couldn't help. The family, of course, was grief-stricken. The coaches were numb with sorrow. And our players were concerned for the family and concerned about the conditioning drills themselves. It was a very tough time for everyone.

*

To keep from being overwhelmed by adversity, I work hard to

keep my priorities in order. The priorities in my life, ranked in descending order, are:

GOD

FAMILY

OTHERS

FOOTBALL

It's easy to come up with such a noble-sounding menu as this. It's another thing entirely when life hands you the bill for your choices.

It's not always been easy to put God first or to maintain my family's priority over the time demands of coaching. I see things I could've done better, others that I should've done differently, and many that I regret. But I'd follow the same path if I had another 50 years in coaching.

Keeping God first is easy when you're successful. The real test comes when adversity strikes. Sometimes the only thing you can do is simply lift your empty cup upward in a defiant affirmation of faith. At other times, you cling to faith because you just don't wish to live otherwise.

The story is told about a group of rabbis held in a Nazi concentration camp during World War II. The camp was a human slaughterhouse. Those who managed to avoid the gas chamber or the operating table endured almost unimaginable brutality. The camp was a mockery of faith in God. And the inevitable questions arose: *How can a just and merciful God permit such cruelty? Why doesn't God intervene?* Faith seemed clearly to count for nothing for these tormented prisoners. The beleaguered rabbis had no good answers for their fellow prisoners.

So the rabbis convened a council in their barracks. The mood was grim. God was put on trial for war crimes against humanity. All sides of the case were presented. No one rushed to judgment. Then, after lengthy deliberation, the stunning verdict was handed down from among those rabbis holding council.

God was found GUILTY.

The prisoners judged that God must take blame for the horrors of the Nazi death camps.

With a rap of the hammer, court was dismissed. There was a moment of dazed silence. The disillusioned rabbis wondered how to conclude a meeting so ominous as this . . . how to go forward and face the next day.

Then one rabbi turned to his colleagues and commanded, *Let us pray.*

Up against the impenetrable mystery of evil, they chose belief over disbelief.

I doubt any of us can fathom the Jewish holocaust of World War II. But we can learn a lot from others about accepting adversity without being crushed by it.

The most important lesson to learn is that tragedy, no matter how great, must never be confused with ultimate defeat.

Denied sight, speech, and hearing, Helen Keller sent this message to the rest of us: *I do not understand the meaning of the darkness. But I have found the overcoming of it.*

※

At the memorial service for Devaughn Darling, teammate Brian Allen got up and made the following remarks:

It makes no sense that D.D. would be here at one moment and gone the next. It makes no sense that at one moment he's a big strong football player and the next moment he'll never play football again. But reality isn't always what we want it to be, or what we think it should be. Reality isn't fair, it's just what it is. Bad stuff happens to good people.

Bad stuff happens to good people.

We all can recite that mantra easily enough. And we observe it more than we'd like. Bad things sometimes happen to good people. Good things sometimes happen to bad people.

Or, to view it from a different angle, one person's good experience is another person's bad experience. I got the job at FSU because another guy got fired. I moved my family to a bigger house, and he had to move his family out of town. It happens all the time. It's part of life. And it sometimes has little to do with how good we are as human beings.

If you wish to be a great leader, then accept down deep inside yourself that life is not fair. You are not owed a great hand to play. But you are given an opportunity, and the strength, to face any adversity that arises.

Adversity will come.

You must decide how you will face it.

A good leader will offer others a path worth following.

✳

When we face adversity during a ballgame, I remind my coaches and players of one thing: DON'T PANIC.

Game time is not the right occasion for philosophical discussions on the problem of evil. Game time demands fast, accurate solutions to problems. And panic is a real problem on the football field.

Panic will make you do things you regret. During a game, it causes players to overplay. They start trying too hard. Order gives way to chaos. Players forget the things we've taught them. Soon they're running 100 percent on emotion.

When players are aggressive and confused at the same time, mistakes multiply.

So before a big game, I prepare my players for the possibility of adversity: *Men, don't worry if we get behind. It's possible, because they've got some great players on that other team. But you're great players, too. So don't panic and think we've got to get it all back in one or two plays. Just do what we've coached you to do.*

If we come back at halftime and indeed are losing the game, I'll remind them: *Men, don't lose your composure.* DON'T LOSE YOUR COMPOSURE. *The game lasts 60 minutes. You just go out there, give your best, and execute plays the way we've practiced them. The rest of it will take care of itself.*

When we face adversity during a game, it's my job as their leader to keep panic from setting in.

Of course, the best defense against confusion and panic is *habit*. If our players have the right habits instilled during practice, they're apt to rely on habit and do the right things when adversity strikes.

But sometimes not even good habits help. In that case, I might try to shock the players by challenging their manhood or their courage. People will ignore adversity if you get 'em mad enough about it.

In the 1994 season finale against Florida, when we came back and scored 28 points in the final 12 minutes for a 31-31 tie, Florida had us down 24-3 at halftime.

The halftime score made the game look closer than it really was. Florida was simply dominating us in our own house. My players had lost their emotion. They sat around the locker room at halftime not knowing what to say. These guys were beyond panic. They were ready to concede.

So just before heading back onto the field, I stood in the midst of my players and offered this message:

Men, listen up. Let's pay good attention.

We're behind 21 points. . . . They make three dadgum plays out there, and we're behind 21 points.

Now you're going to find out what you're made of.

You did not fight that first half. Florida is going to take that film back and look at that film and LAUGH *where they whipped your butts today. They're gonna laugh at you!*

Hey, if you won't fight, don't go back into the game this next half. IF YOU AIN'T GONNA FIGHT, DON'T YOU DARE GO BACK IN THE DANG BALLGAME!

We gotta have great protection. We gotta have great blocking. We gotta have great running. We gotta have great catching. We gotta have great pass rush . . . SACKING . . . HITTING. *They out-hit us that first half. That's one thing I don't like.*

You're gonna find out what you're made of. LET'S GO. DO IT!

I wasn't looking to inspire them to win. All I wanted to do was get their minds off the problem and get focused again on good technique and hard-nosed football.

✳

Public opinion is yet another form of adversity. I ignore it. And I tell my secretary never to bring bad mail into my office. She does a pretty good job, and I remain happy. When adversity strikes, move to the front and take the point. That's where the leader belongs. As Bear Bryant said, *Don't try to hide behind anything or anybody. They're going to find you anyway.*

25
CHANGING WITH
THE TIMES

If short haircuts and polite manners were the keys to success, Army and Navy would play for the national championship every year.

Change is inevitable.

Change we must.

But change is scary – especially when we must change a cherished belief or a long-standing custom.

Like the plant that outgrows its shallow soil, life periodically requires us to be uprooted and replanted in deeper soil. There we will flourish and grow larger. But the betwixt-and-between phase – that period of uncertainty between uprooting and replanting – is scary. The shallow soil may be inadequate, but at least it's familiar. The place we're going is unknown. Hence our fear of change and our urge to resist it.

But if fear wins out, we get left behind. Life itself moves inexorably forward. Those who resist are left to wither and die.

The Bible teaches us to *fear not*. That's a good starting point for any aspiring leader.

＊

I'm not too proud to change. I like to win too much.

Some say the ability to change with the times is the main reason for my continued success over the years. That's an exaggerated assessment, but there is a measure of truth to it.

Some of my leadership methods *have* changed over the years as I adapted to new circumstances. I haven't changed my moral values, mind you. Those aren't open to negotiation. But otherwise if something works better, I'll try it.

I was raised on conservative football. Three yards and a cloud of dust. At South Georgia College and Samford, I mixed trick plays into my game plan – such as reverses and passes back across the field – but my younger years were basically governed by old-style football. I ran the ball. On third and long, I considered the pass.

I imitated the greats of my era: Leahy at Notre Dame, Bryant at Alabama, Dodd at Georgia Tech. Any coach worth his salt taught smash-mouth football in those days.

Then, in 1963, Bill Peterson hired me to coach receivers at Florida State. We didn't have a lot of talented players on our team – at least, not in comparison to our competition. So Peterson developed a passing attack. If we couldn't play smash-mouth, maybe we could outfinesse them through the air. Pass on first down. Pass on third and short. Pass whenever the defense expected a run.

It worked. We beat Oklahoma in the Gator Bowl in 1964, and passing was the key to our success.

The scales fell off and I began to see with new eyes.

When I played college ball, I was a small 155-pound quarterback. I made the small college All-American team by being quicker and stealthier than the bigger guys I played against. Small guys like me had to be cunning.

Up until 1963, *cunning* meant trick plays. Catch the opposition off guard. Use smoke and mirrors to exploit their tendencies.

Then Bill Peterson's passing philosophy reminded me of something inherent in my own nature. Why not pass when they least expect it?

Some people say that if you pass the ball, three things can happen, two of which are bad. You can be intercepted. You can throw incomplete. Or – and this is the only good thing – you can complete the pass.

The late coach Woody Hayes of Ohio State offered an expanded version of this old saw. He said that *three* bad things can happen when you pass. His addition to the list was . . . *getting fired!*

That conservative coaching philosophy was self-evident to all of us back in the '50s and '60s. Somehow we just neglected to analyze our assumptions about the running game. But Bill Peterson's passing attack provided me with the analytical tools I needed.

Passing appears to be risky only because the ball is in the air. To an old-style coach, *letting go of the ball* is scary. But I realized that

(i) if the receiver knows where he is going, and (ii) if the quarterback knows where to throw the ball – and can get it there – then passing poses no bigger risk than running. A coach who is willing to balance running with passing, or vice-versa, can win. Just look at how many national championships have been won by Miami, Florida State, and Florida over the past fifteen years.

Nowadays, my philosophy is to favor the run or the pass, depending on what the opposing defense gives me. If they crowd the line of scrimmage, I'll pass until their tongues hang out. If they back off too deep, I'll run, run, run.

And by the way, no disrespect to Coach Hayes, but coaches have lost more games from fumbles than from interceptions.

✳

My leadership style has undergone three major modifications over the past 35 years, all of which represent my efforts to change with the times.

1. My perception of coaching authority has changed.

In my youth, a player never questioned his coach. Such audacity was unthinkable. Challenging a coach's orders was the surest way to get kicked off the team. That's the mentality I took into coaching in the early '50s, and I didn't change much well into the '60s.

In the 1970s, however, player attitudes began to change. I think part of it was due to the Civil Rights Movement. Black players had become an obvious presence on the field by 1970, and our society was learning to take African-American culture seriously. Black and white athletes, along with their coaches, probably adapted to this new blended family much quicker than the rest of society. Gee, when the integration of black athletes in major college football first began in the south, alumni would often ask how many blacks I had on my team. The question came so frequently that I developed a stock response: *I don't know. I don't count.*

Other social events also affected player attitudes. We had student demonstrations against the war in Vietnam and the whole counter-culture movement centered out in California. Then Watergate hit in the early '70s, about the time the women's movement was getting underway. It was also a time when our players began questioning "The System." They stood up for their rights. When told to do something, some of them began to ask why.

I was not schooled in cultural analysis, but I could see that the world of my childhood was rapidly coming to an end. Old-style coaching was on its way out. Some of my colleagues couldn't bring themselves to embrace these changes. They held tenaciously to the past, and many of them lost credibility with their players. If I wished to retain my own credibility and authority, I would have to take a different tack. I would need to explain to players why we do what we do. I'd need to show them how my system works to their benefit.

This change in my leadership style didn't occur all at once. It has slowly evolved over the past 30 years. But I first began feeling the pressure back in the 1960s. If I lost the ability to relate to my players, I couldn't coach them effectively, which in my mind translated into losses on game day. I hate to lose. Change was my only viable option.

2. My treatment of players changed.

I was probably one of the first major college coaches to allow long hair, earrings, and tattoos among my players when they first became popular. I don't like them, mind you, because I come from a different time. Some singer caught my attention on the radio when he sang, *I wish I didn't know now what I didn't know then.* That's how I feel about these body piercings and tattoos. We just didn't do that stuff in my early years, and I wish people wouldn't do it now. But kids make a big deal about it these days, so I make concessions.

I still don't allow beards or scraggly facial hair. Our players are told to look neat and clean. And we will never take votes on whether to hold practice in August. But I've learned to bend on issues that don't challenge my basic moral values or undermine the integrity of my program.

3. My moral sensitivities have changed.

I was raised in a conservative protestant religious environment. While I've never been pushy about my religious convictions, I've held onto some strong personal beliefs that have not changed and will not change in essence. My mother and father taught me a lot about love, discipline, faith, determination, and the deep satisfaction that comes from living a morally good life. A religious compass has guided my life ever since leaving home as a young man.

And I always wanted that kind of environment in my football program. I would not, and still will not, hire someone whose fundamental convictions are at odds with my own. And I will not hire an immoral person under any circumstance.

But I have learned that sometimes you must make allowances because of changing social conditions.

Divorce is a case in point. Throughout most of my career, I would not hire a coach who was divorced. I didn't believe in divorce. My convictions were so strong that, as I mentioned earlier, I once dismissed a coach because he divorced his wife.

In retrospect, I regret having done this. Divorce is more common today than in earlier years. The whole concept of marriage seems to be undergoing social redefinition. I now realize that my attitude toward divorce was influenced as much by social convention as it was by religious conviction. So I've held onto my religious conviction but have negotiated on the social convention side. As society has become more tolerant, I have become more tolerant.

But not in all respects.

We may refer to alcoholism today as *chemical dependence*, but drunkenness under any name will get a guy dismissed from my staff. So will sexual misconduct and disloyalty, which are moral issues to the core.

✳

Good morale is very important to long-term success. Year in and year out, the people in your organization must believe that all the little things that have made you successful are still important and still require their best efforts.

I watch attentively for anything that might undermine team morale. And if I can make some changes that help team morale, I'll make them.

Louis Farrakhan's "Million Man March" back in 1995 really affected our black athletes at the time. The march was scheduled to take place in Washington in the middle of our football season.

Georgia Tech was next on our schedule, and they posed a real threat. We needed to make the most of every minute in practice. Some of our black athletes, however, felt they should be permitted to attend the march in Washington. I wasn't sure what to do. If too many guys left, we'd probably lose the game to Georgia Tech. And I was afraid they all might go. I eventually suggested that they select one representative on the team to attend the march. The players found that agreeable.

A number of our black athletes went a step further and said we should call off practice on the day of the march. Some players made this request out of conviction. I suspect some others went along just to get out of practice. My first impulse was to refuse the request. But I feared such a decision might split our team by appearing to be racially motivated. I ended up calling off practice, with the proviso that we'd make up the practice time later in the week, which we did.

We won the game against Georgia Tech.

Some coaches at other schools did not call off practice on the day of the march, and some had real problems.

✳

I keep up with new trends in my profession.

My basic offensive scheme has evolved over the past 50 years through the following stages: Wing-T, Option, I-formation, Shotgun, No Huddle, and Spread Offense. I try to stay on the front edge of change. The first coach to use the wishbone attack won games. The last coach to use it got fired.

My motive for these changes has always been winning.

We switched to the shotgun back in 1992 when Charlie Ward was our quarterback. I think Charlie must've averaged about three interceptions a game during the first half of that season. Some of our own fans started booing and wanted us to replace him. We were running out of the I-formation. Charlie was taking the snap from under center.

During those first few games of the '92 season, as the coaches reviewed each week's game film, we noticed that Charlie was much more accurate when he didn't have to turn his back to the line of scrimmage. Quarterbacks who take the snap while under center must turn and run backwards before turning again to look downfield for their receivers. What if we put Charlie about seven yards deep and let the center snap the ball back to him? After all, whenever we went to our two minute offense late in a game, that's what we had Charlie do, and he did it well. Why not play the entire game with that offensive formation? Charlie could keep his eyes on that defense from the very beginning. Of course, our offense would also lose the element of surprise. Every one of those big defensive linemen would know right where the ball was going each play – into Charlie's hands. There would be no disguised hand-offs and misdirection plays to the fullback or halfback – at least, not in any traditional sense. Charlie would have the ball in his hands each time we snapped it. And he stood too deep in the backfield to attempt any traditional-style hand-off to the halfback. If we went to the shotgun, the entire success of our offense would depend on Charlie's ability to make good decisions on every play.

Well, we made our decision in the second half of the Georgia Tech game, down 24-10 with ten minutes to go. Charlie took over the game and we won in the final minutes.

Our decision proved even more valuable than we first realized. In the shotgun formation, Charlie's completion rate improved dramatically. His uncanny field vision and elusive running ability – both of which we had seen on the practice field on busted plays – became the norm during games. We won the remainder of our games that season.

The next year we stayed in the shotgun formation and added another wrinkle – no huddles before the plays. When a play was over, Charlie would rush up to the line of scrimmage, look over the defense, signal the play he wanted to call, and then take the snap back in that shotgun formation. Defenses didn't have time to substitute players or take a breather. We created a lot of mismatches to our advantage. We also captured our first national championship, and Charlie won the Heisman Trophy.

✳

All the changes I've made have been for pragmatic reasons. If something new works better for our program, then I'll try it.

The objective is to be one of the first to change, not one of the last.

26
AGE—THE CAVEAT

←——————————————→

The goal is not to become the youngest leader
in America, but the oldest.

Age counts in leadership.

When you're young, you lack experience and credibility. No young leader can bypass the learning process, so don't feel like you've got to have the wisdom of Solomon. You don't – BUT YOU CAN STILL BE AN EFFECTIVE LEADER.

Just work hard to do what is right, as best you know how, and be patient. Experience is on its way.

When I first started at South Georgia College in 1955, I hired an assistant who was three years younger than me. We had grown up together as friends in Birmingham, Alabama. Neither of us thought of me as the leader. There were no ego issues because we were both too young and too poor to afford egos. We worked hard together and were paid little for our services. We were compatriots in every good sense of the term, like Lewis and Clark on their expedition of discovery.

That's the way it is when you're young. If you're worried that people aren't showing you enough respect or granting you enough authority, you're leading with the wrong foot.

＊

My advice to young leaders is:

1. Don't pretend to be someone you're not. Just be yourself and do your job as best you can.

2. Focus on character issues.

You can earn respect no matter what age you are. If people perceive your dedication to do what is right, they'll cut you some slack when you do it wrong. So strive to be a good person and set a good example. Experience will happen to you over the years, and that experience can make you much wiser than you are now. Be diligent in your attention to detail. Develop the habits of good leadership now, and later on they'll become instinctive.

I think of the Israelites at the Red Sea. They fled Egypt with the pharaoh's army hot on their heels. When they got to the Red Sea, the escape effort appeared temporary and futile. They didn't know what would happen next. But they were where they were supposed to be, and that's what mattered. They had done what was asked of them up to that point. God took care of the rest.

3. Learn from your mistakes. But be sure to learn the right lessons.

Young leaders are so worried about credibility that they oftentimes are unwilling to acknowledge their own mistakes. Mistakes might make them appear as what they really are – namely, someone on the front end of the learning curve.

Just try to be honest and humble when you make mistakes. Accept that you'll make some bad decisions. Your dark side may want to always pin the blame on others. Resist this temptation. If you make a mistake, then look for ways that will prevent you from making the same mistake again.

The biggest mistake a young leader can make is to continue practicing a mistake. Football has made that point amply clear to me.

4. Be patient and let time do its work.

When I was a young 23-year-old coach fresh out of college, the students on campus called me "Bobby." That made sense because we'd just been classmates the year before. Then one day, not too many years later, college-age kids began calling me "Mr. Bowden" and addressing me with "Yes, sir" and "No, sir." It felt odd, because I still considered myself a young man. Yet a gulf had opened between us because of our age difference. Certain people now looked upon me as an adult. As I got older, the gulf got wider. And with it came a certain measure of credibility in the eyes of others.

You've just got to let time take care of that for you. I never insisted that my staff, or the students on campus, refer to me as "Coach Bowden." It just happened naturally and appropriately on its own time schedule.

CONCLUSION

Football isn't life and death.

My close friends know that faith is the cornerstone of my life. Everything I do is done with the aim of obedience to God. Nothing I say in this book should be taken outside the context of faith, because faith in God is the driving force of my whole existence. I firmly believe that God lies behind whatever success I've had and whatever influence I've managed to impart.

Two of my sons have become Division I head football coaches. Terry took command at Auburn University in 1993 before joining ABC Sports in 1999. His older brother Tommy accepted the head coaching job at Tulane University in 1997 and then became the head coach at Clemson University in 1999.

I sent both sons a copy of my "Thirty-Five Rules." These rules have guided my actions since I first became a Division I head coach at West Virginia University in 1970. The rules haven't changed.

Here they are. You'll find them heavily peppered with my religious convictions, for which I offer no apology:

✗ Get mentally tough or get out of coaching.

✗ Fear no man. Fear only God.

✗ Face the issue . . . now!

✗ Never allow success to make you lax or undisciplined.

✗ Don't lose your guts. If you believe in your plan, carry it out regardless.

✗ You may be wrong, but you are the boss.

✗ Don't forget the Alabama-Tennessee game of 1966. (Bear Bryant's team was tied 14-14 with Tennessee with about one minute to play. Alabama had the ball inside Tennessee's 10-yard line and needed only a field goal to win. On fourth down, a panicked Ken Stabler threw the ball out of bounds to stop the clock. Tennessee got the ball on downs, and an easy Alabama victory ended up instead as an embarrassing tie.) The moral: Even great coaches and great players can make dumb mistakes.

✗ The only thing to fear is fear itself.
　　　　　　　　　～ Franklin Delano Roosevelt

✗ Trust in the Lord with all your heart . . . and He will direct your path.
　　　　　　　　　～ Prov. 3:5-6

✘ If you can't stand the heat, get out of the kitchen.
~ Harry S. Truman

✘ You do not have because you do not ask.
~ Jas. 4:2

✘ The greatest mistake of all is to continue practicing a mistake.

✘ Benjamin Franklin, Thomas Edison, Winston Churchill, Franklin Roosevelt, Blanton Collier, Paul Brown, and Vince Lombardi all made mistakes, but they shook them off to succeed. At times they were down right losers.

✘ Depend upon the Lord and He will grant your heart's desire.
~ Ps. 37:4

✘ Christ calls us to be servants, not masters.

✘ Have I not commanded you? Be strong and of good courage. Be not afraid, and do not be dismayed. For the Lord your God is with you wherever you go.
~ Josh. 1:9

✘ Why worry . . . when you can pray?

✘ Team rights supercede individual rights.

✘ I will never leave you or forsake you.
~ Heb. 13:5

✘ God doesn't sponsor flunkies. If you are one of His, He will want you to succeed.

✗ Responsibility without authority will result in failure.

✗ He that has knowledge spares his words. . . . Even a fool, when he holds his peace, is counted wise.
~ Prov. 17:27-28

✗ Be confident in this one thing – that God, who began a good work in you, will complete it.
~ Phil. 1:6

✗ No man who puts his hand to the plow and then looks back is fit for the kingdom of God.
~ Luke 9:62

✗ When two partners always agree, one of them is not necessary.

✗ Good steel must go through the hottest fire.

✗ Alibis are just another way to get free of blame by way of excuse.

✗ We ask for favors. God gives us opportunities.

✗ Christ was tough-minded but tender-hearted.
~ William James

✗ If you were being tried in court for being a Christian, would there be enough evidence to convict you?

✗ Lord, help my words to be gracious and tender today, for tomorrow I may have to eat them.

✗ If a dog won't do what you teach him to do, then teach

him to do what he can do.

✗ It is better to fail in a cause that will ultimately succeed than to succeed in a cause that will ultimately fail.

✗ Learn from others but don't try imitating them. You're not them.

✗ I don't believe in playing without a scoreboard.